Embracing the Chaos

THE RESOURCE ROOM
CHURCH HOUSE
9 THE CLOSE
WINCHESTER
SO23 9LS

WINCHESTER SCHOOL OF MISSION

07328

Embracing the Chaos

Theological Responses to AIDS

Edited by
JAMES WOODWARD

First published in Great Britain 1990

SPCK
Holy Trinity Church
Marylebone Road
London NW1 4DU

© James Woodward, Peter Baelz, Andrew Henderson, Leslie Houlden,
Grace Jantzen, Kenneth Leech, Sara Maitland, Edward Norman,
Stephen Pattison, Mark Pryce, Jeanette Renouf 1990

All rights reserved. No part of this book may be reproduced or
transmitted in any form or by any means, electronic or
mechanical, including photocopying, recording, or by any
information storage and retrieval system, without permission
in writing from the publisher.

We are grateful to Faber and Faber Ltd and Harcourt Brace
Jovanovich, Orlando, for permission to quote an extract
from 'Little Gidding' by T. S. Eliot, in *Collected Poems.
1909–62* (Faber 1963).

*For my parents,
Colin and Patricia,
with love and thanks*

British Library Cataloguing in Publication Data

Embracing the chaos.
1. Man. AIDS – Christian viewpoints
I. Woodward, James, *1961* –
261.561

ISBN 0-281-04465-1

Printed in Great Britain by
WBC Print Ltd, Bristol and Maesteg

Contents

Contributors   vii

Foreword
Richard Harries, Bishop of Oxford   ix

Acknowledgements   x

Introduction
James Woodward   1

1. To the Churches with Love from the Lighthouse
   Stephen Pattison   8

   Nigel Sheldrick   20

2. AIDS, Shame and Suffering
   Grace Jantzen   22

   Lloyd   32

3. Members One of Another
   Andrew Henderson   35

   John Shine   45

4. New Showings: God Revealed in Friendship
   Mark Pryce   48

   Adrian   57

5. 'The Carnality of Grace': Sexuality, Spirituality and
   Pastoral Ministry
   Kenneth Leech   59

   David Randall   69

6. Order and Chaos: The Church and Sexuality
   Jeanette Renouf   72

   Sebastian   80

7. AIDS and the Will of God
   Edward Norman   82

   Victoria   90

8. Is Health a Gospel Imperative?
   Sara Maitland   92

   Anna   101

9. In a Biblical Perspective
   Leslie Houlden   103

10. What sort of world? What sort of God?
   Peter Baelz   109

   'And who is my neighbour?'   116

Contributors

JAMES WOODWARD was born in Durham in 1961 and has studied theology in London and Cambridge. He worked at St Christopher's Hospice and Consett Parish Church before his appointment as Chaplain to the Bishop of Oxford in 1987. He is presently engaged in researching appropriate theological responses to HIV/AIDS.

STEPHEN PATTISON is Secretary of the Central Birmingham Community Health Council and a recognized lecturer in Theology in the University of Birmingham. He is author of *A Critique of Pastoral Care* (SCM 1988) and *Alive and Kicking: Towards a Practical Theology of Illness and Healing* (SCM 1989).

GRACE JANTZEN has studied at the Universities of Saskatchewan, Calgary and Oxford. She lectures in Philosophy of Religion at King's College, London, and is an editor of *Theology*. Her books include *Julian of Norwich: Mystic and Theologian* (SPCK 1987).

ANDREW HENDERSON trained concurrently for ordination and psychiatric social work. His career in London Social Services concluded with eleven years as Director of Social Services for Kensington and Chelsea. Following a period as Director of the St Marylebone Centre for Healing and Counselling he now chiefly gives his time to London Lighthouse where he chairs the Management Council.

MARK PRYCE was born in Shropshire in 1960. He read English at the University of Sussex and trained for the Anglican ministry at Westcott House. He is now working in a parish in the Black Country. His meditation on St Matthew's Passion in the light of AIDS has been widely acclaimed (see *Christian*, September/October 1987).

KENNETH LEECH has been Director of the Runnymede Trust, an educational unit concerned with race and racism in the UK, since 1987. He has spent the largest part of his ministry in the East End of London, and was Rector of St Matthew's, Bethnal Green, from 1974 to 1980. He founded the Soho Drugs Group in 1967 and Centrepoint in 1969. He is the author of numerous books including *Youthquake, Soul Friend, True Prayer, True God, Spirituality and Pastoral Care* and *Struggle in Babylon: Racism in the Cities and Churches of Britain*, all published by Sheldon Press.

JEANETTE RENOUF is Advisor for Pastoral Care and Counselling to the Diocese of Southwark. She has been a clinical psychotherapist for the past fifteen years, working in that capacity, and in pastoral care, for the past eight years as a missionary of the Episcopal Church, USA.

EDWARD NORMAN is a writer and broadcaster on historical and religious themes. His books include *Christianity and the World Order* (OUP 1979) and

Christianity in the Southern Hemisphere (OUP 1981). He was for many years Dean of Peterhouse, Cambridge, and is now Chaplain of Christ Church College, Canterbury.

SARA MAITLAND has written novels and short stories as well as being involved with feminist theology and journalism. In 1983 she published *A Map of the New Country* (Routledge), a classic study of feminism and Christianity. She lives in East London and is currently working on the libretto for an opera about AIDS.

LESLIE HOULDEN is Professor of Theology at King's College, London, and an editor of *Theology*. He was a curate in Leeds and later taught Theology in Chichester, Oxford and London. He has published many commentaries and books on the interface of Christian belief and biblical studies, including *Connections: the Integration of Theology and Faith* (SCM 1986).

PETER BAELZ worked in parishes in Birmingham before teaching theology in Cambridge and Oxford. He was Regius Professor of Moral and Pastoral Theology at Oxford from 1972 to 1979 and Dean of Durham from 1980 to 1988. He is author of numerous books including *Prayer and Providence* and *The Forgotten Dream*. He now lives in retirement in Wales.

Foreword

AIDS evokes a wide range of emotions and one of the virtues of this book is that it allows that range to display itself without false selectivity or partiality. Feelings about disease and disfigurement, sex and death, futility and friendship are present without sentimentalization or false romanticism. There is both bitterness and vitality. For this is a book that is rooted in experience. The main chapters are punctuated by autobiographical sketches of people who have been diagnosed as HIV positive. The chapters themselves are related both pastorally and philosophically to this experience. For this is also a book that strives towards theology; a theology that is groping and tentative but nonetheless theology. It has been written to help the Church formulate for itself the mind of Christ in response to the AIDS crisis and, in particular, to the individuals who are afflicted. Some churchpeople will not find it a comfortable book to read. It questions and criticizes many of our accustomed attitudes. But if read attentively it genuinely questions our unthinking assumptions and inherited presuppositions.

It is a book that more than most has moments of real personal vulnerability. In return, the authors can expect of us, the readers, the self-discipline to put aside quick condemnation, and a willingness to ponder the pondered experience in these pages.

There is bitter honesty here both about disease and the Church. There is also gospel, the gospel of those who, through this crisis, have learnt how to live. I am reminded of King Lear who, stripped of everything and utterly humiliated, discovers the overriding worth of human relationship. Lear says to Cordelia:

> Come, let's away to prison;
> We two alone will sing like birds i' the cage:
> When thou dost ask me blessing, I'll kneel down,
> And ask of thee forgiveness: so we'll live,
> And pray, and sing . . .
> And take upon 's the mystery of things,
> As if we were God's spies.

We can be grateful to James Woodward for devising a structure to the book which holds reality and reflection together; and for attracting such honest, brave and thoughtful contributions.

Richard Oxon.
October 1989

Acknowledgements

My thanks are due to a number of people. My involvement in this project would not have been possible without the support of the Bishop of Oxford, who generously gave me the space to read, reflect and to give time to all the contributors. I am grateful, too, that he has provided the Foreword to this collection. Andrew Henderson and David Randall allowed me to develop links with some of those living with HIV through CARA (Care and Resources for People Affected by AIDS/HIV) and have given me their support and encouragement throughout. Stephen Pattison, my research supervisor, and Leslie Houlden stimulated thought and were always ready to offer theological tutorials! My thanks to friends for insight and support: Martin Roper, Penny Casemore and Paul Keene. My thanks to all the contributors who were patient with their editor and who managed to keep to deadlines. A special word of thanks to Mark for his friendship and support.

My own life has been particularly enriched and changed by my engagement with those living and dying with HIV and AIDS. Only very small parts of our conversations are recorded here but they represent very significant themes of listening and sharing that have helped me to glimpse something of what healing and real despair are about in the face of HIV. I thank them all for allowing me into their trust and giving me time for many questions. I have learned much from them.

Finally thanks to Philip Law of SPCK for editorial support; to Avril Rastelli, Rosalind Beuzeval and Rachel Enock for typing.

James Woodward
Oxford, January 1990

Introduction

James Woodward

The Christian Churches' response to AIDS has been a mixture of constructive and divisive engagement with the people, groups and issues that surround the subject. This is hardly surprising: faced with a disease that forces us to face the reality of sex, disability, disfigurement and death, we are bound to feel a mixture of fear, ignorance, disgust, hostility and embarrassed compassion. At the least we avert our eyes and at the worst we want to push AIDS as far away as possible. How could any socially responsible group's response be otherwise? Nobody wants to face questions about death, disease and sexuality, except perhaps those involved in care or who are working through these particular issues for themselves—we want to take them for granted. It has probably never been otherwise. Could one then expect any response to AIDS from the Church to be anything other than mixed and problematical?

The prevailing response voiced by some conservative Christians continues to suggest that AIDS is God's punishment on those homosexuals and intravenous drug users who do not obey God's law. With the Churches remaining largely silent, society can hardly be faulted for assuming that this perspective is representative of the whole Christian community. The sense that AIDS has entered into a perceived scene of moral chaos is shared by many in Church and society. Many have used AIDS as the opportunity to prove a whole series of negative assertions about our culture. This perspective emerges from any attempts to answer the question, 'What is the meaning of AIDS?' Has AIDS got some profound, hidden meaning that reveals truth about life? Or is it simply an opportunistic infection that serves to reinforce our sense of the randomness of life and our powerlessness? It is important to decide from which standpoint or perspective theological reflection should start.

Among those who have chosen to involve themselves in the pastoral care of people living with HIV are some who have decided that much of theology is either wrong and harmful or has no particular part to play in pastoral care. To their credit individuals and organizations have provided a non-judgemental approach to compassionate care of persons with HIV and their families, partners and friends. Ministry from this perspective is a matter of doing and not thinking. There is a deep commitment to unconditional loving and care with no sense that theology might have anything to contribute to the quality of that care. Aspects of this approach draw upon particular methods of 'client-centred' counselling.[1] The primary focus of attention and the main body of material used for learning are the individual's experience. Here the framework is descriptive rather than prescriptive: it arises out of attention to the self struggling to come to terms with HIV. From this perspective much of explicit theology becomes irrelevant and only causes problems, particularly in relation to the evaluation of the moral aspects of sexual activity.[2]

Amidst all these responses, any serious attempt to struggle with the moral, ethical and theological issues that AIDS is precipitating, has been almost wholly missing. This volume of essays seeks to open up some of the range of issues that AIDS raises.

Our subject is of course one topic among many in the pastoral area. Few authors seem willing or able to elaborate a full theology of pastoral care, in an age liberated from authoritarian, paternalistic text-book answers and more inclined to the pragmatism which relies upon client-centred counselling. Although some authors have attempted to define in a theoretical way what pastoral care is, it is unclear where the boundaries of the subject lie. There are no coherent underlying assumptions linking the increasing volume of literature on pastoral studies. What are the aims, methodology—and theology—of pastoral care?[3]

This may partly reflect the infancy of the subject; it will take time for a body of scholarly conventions to grow. Perhaps, too, it reflects the difficulty Christian women and men have always had in attempting to provide theological reflection on particular practical issues and problems.

Yet the experience of drawing together the reflections in this book reinforces my conviction that we need to recover our commitment to theology and its place in shaping and forming the human person. Theology, as here understood, is not so much a rigid collection of principles, concepts and history, as a way of exploring life in the light of our sense of faith in God.[4] It is a questioning, exploratory enquiry into life, a dynamic process that should engage the person on every level.

There is a sense in which there is nothing specific about AIDS that raises new theological questions. There are the obvious questions about the nature of God and the relationship between God and the world; how God acts in history; questions about the origin of evil and suffering, innocence and guilt. AIDS challenges us to think about how we should live and exercise our freedom and responsibility. There is the question of death, and above all AIDS raises issues of justice. In view of this it is reasonable to ask whether theology or a particular type of theology can help us to live creatively with these challenges. What kind of theology can facilitate growth into and through the experience of AIDS?

The fundamental presupposition of this book is that the Church has an opportunity to recover the theological basis of its pastoral response to AIDS in a way that can extend compassion, promote justice, and offer support, nurture and hope. Pastoral care is always related to faith in so far as it can and should reveal what the community of faith believes about God, the mission of the Church and the meaning of discipleship. At the same time it is also true that events and experience affect our beliefs about God, ecclesiology and discipleship.

It was with these ideas in mind that I approached a variety of individuals to ask them to explore how theology might help us to find our way through AIDS in a liberating way. I was clear that a number of issues had to be tackled and some particular bad understandings and meanings explained. I drew on a number of people who had already some experience of reflecting on AIDS and working closely with those persons living with HIV. Integral to the whole exercise was a commitment on the part of those who were reflecting and thinking to listen to and learn from those persons who were living with HIV. If theology is a continuous and critical conversation between the community of faith and its perceptions of reality, then we had to give a particular authority to the experience that derives from the hopes and fears of those who were living and dying with HIV. A meeting was therefore arranged between contributors to this book and people living with HIV. It was a remarkable experience for the whole group as we were led into richer perceptions as well as new problems and challenges.

In addition to this I was privileged to have conversations with other people with HIV, some of which were recorded and edited and are here printed alongside the essays. Each person speaks about their experience and what life means for them so that theology here is earthed and contextualized in the experience of HIV. This willingness to share in each other's stories enabled us to glimpse the experience of a theology that could support, listen, change, evoke response and create movements towards people who were striving towards a sense of inclusiveness, mutuality and creativity in the face of HIV. The result is a very diverse, overlapping and sometimes contradictory collection of reflections. They unravel the love and joy, support and care, devastation and pain, loss and bereavement of those engaging with HIV and AIDS.

In the first essay, Stephen Pattison sets the scene with a personal theological reflection on the meeting of contributors to this book and people with HIV that took place in July 1989. He wrestles with some of the challenges that emerged from the conversations, and captures something of the experience of openness, honesty and trust that was shared. He takes some of the themes of this experience and interrogates the institutional Church. How do we face the chaos and death of HIV? Can the Churches ever hope to work through their latent prejudices towards those who have come to be recognized as different, and stigmatized and unacceptable?

Grace Jantzen explores the relationship of shame and suffering in AIDS. She shows us that AIDS and HIV offer us the opportunity to rediscover Christ; an opportunity to identify ourselves with the love and dignity, suffering and fear in all this human tragedy. She explores too whether our present theological theories about suffering are not our way of avoiding fear, of insulating ourselves from reality.

Andrew Henderson brings his experience of being at the forefront of the response to AIDS in London to explore what the practical implications are for the Churches in relation to AIDS. He argues that there are good reasons why the Churches find AIDS difficult, but, once faced together, these can provide many opportunities for growth and community. Mark Pryce explores aspects of our response through story and dialogue with the Bible. What models of ministry should characterize our pastoral involvement with those who live most vulnerably in the face of HIV? How do we think about God? What do friendship and solidarity mean?

Kenneth Leech develops these themes as he works out what it means practically for us to affirm incarnation, a religion which places high value on the flesh, on the physical. If this is so, why do we find it so hard to deal with issues of human sexuality? This essay challenges us all to integrate our sexuality and spirituality, and to take our sexual nature seriously as a means of moving towards God and each other. How can we become better pastors as we struggle for personal and political liberation?

Jeanette Renouf provides the book with the perspective and insights of a psychotherapist: Why do we have so many problems when we face questions about sexuality? If the function of religion is often seen as maintaining security and order against chaos and threat, then how might the Church develop a theology of sexuality that supports and affirms diversity? Is the Church prepared to accept responsibility for the pain and anger that many gay men and women feel? She reminds us that we need to change the way we deal with sexuality so that the Church can be a place where people share their vulnerability and their search for healing.

Edward Norman explores how far we can view the mind of God in illness. The sense that AIDS has entered into the world's moral chaos still pervades some of the writing on the subject: writers, broadcasters, politicians still need to use AIDS to prove a series of negative assumptions about our culture. Nowhere is this more apparent than in some Christian reflections on illness. This essay also puts the case for a change in Christian attitudes to sexuality in a pervasive and challenging manner.

Sara Maitland shares her experience of standing alongside a friend who takes the HIV antibody test. Sara challenges us to face our horror and fear and denial of death in the face of AIDS. She argues that faced with illness we glamorize and dramatize it in inappropriate ways. How are we to construct meaning around AIDS? What kind of God can we hope to believe in? Are those suffering to be viewed as heroes or victims?

Leslie Houlden picks up this theme in relation to the construction of the death and resurrection of Jesus. What biblical principles are there for interpreting and understanding disastrous elements and episodes in our lives? What does salvation mean for us? How do we find the truth of life amidst the challenges and conflicts of AIDS?

Finally, Peter Baelz has assessed the particular strengths and weaknesses of the reflections gathered together.

The short accounts of personal experiences are an important and integral part of the theological work of the book. They are partial, open-ended, spoken pieces drawn together in order to let those living with HIV speak for themselves. They overlap, challenge and contradict some of the essays, but above all they share something of what it feels like to struggle with this devastating virus. These conversations, the challenges and explorations must continue as we struggle to develop an appropriate theology that informs, supports and deepens compassion.

I once asked a health educator what he thought the Church could do about AIDS. He replied, 'Keep out of the way'. Pastoral care can damage as well as help, abuse as well as support and the Church needs to be aware of how marginal many of its conversations can be to the wider community. The Church must share with others in its responsibility for the failure to respond creatively to AIDS. Fears about sexuality and mortality have been revealed, and further the basic problems of homophobia, racism and sexism emerge to expose prejudice and foster isolation. These are our starting points as we attempt to set the agenda for pastoral care. All pastoral care must be open-ended as well as open-eyed: being involved with people touched by HIV can be a controversial activity! This involvement must accept and acknowledge failures and build upon guiding principles so that the tragedy can be embraced and redeemed.

The scope and seriousness of AIDS cannot be overestimated. This disease threatens millions of individuals no matter their age, sex, race or geographical locality. There is a good deal of controversy over the calculation of the cumulative number of AIDS cases and those who have been diagnosed as being HIV positive. In the UK to date (November 1989) there have been a total of 2779 cases of people with full-blown AIDS and 1465 deaths. Estimates of those infected with the virus in the UK range from 30,000 to 100,000. The World Health Organization estimates that by 1995 up to 50 million people will have been infected with the virus. The precise numbers are difficult to estimate; what is certain is that millions of people will continue to be affected by this crisis as it evolves and progresses. This book can be an important contribution to helping Churches and society identify and respond to the ethical, spiritual and theological issues that AIDS raises.

Words and actions, theory and practice must always belong together. The Church must continue to engage in dialogue with people living with HIV so that all may be empowered to confront the challenges presented by AIDS. This dialogue must form the basis for our commitment to protect human rights and encourage government to make proper health care provision for those in need.[5] The gospel compels us to care for people who are sick, oppressed, or dispossessed and this must extend to our sisters and brothers in Africa where AIDS has exposed the severe inadequacy of their system of health provision.[6] Above all the challenge to disseminate clear information about the virus will continue to be the main way of preventing its spread. The Church could have an important role to play in supporting explicit preventative education programmes. The Church could have a significant role to play in approaching this process of education at a symbolic and non-cognitive level.[7] The tradition is rich in resources that can provide metaphors, meanings and explanations that can deepen insight and evoke response and transformation.

The prospect and tasks of responding to AIDS may well appear to be daunting and overwhelming. This volume bears witness to the growth that listening, sharing and struggling with the experience can bring. It is a step towards developing an approach and methods that articulate an integrated theology. This theology must attempt to articulate a vision of God's presence in the world and through our experience, relationships and understandings. It must attempt to provide a map or framework that can make sense of HIV and the rich ambiguities that surround morality, sex and death. AIDS is a crisis and an opportunity for us to deepen our understanding so that we can support and care; to create communities where inclusiveness, interdependence, creativity and change are shared for the salvation of all. Theology must open itself up to AIDS so that it can transform the tragedy and despair.

NOTES

1. For an example of this approach see Gerard Egan, *The Skilled Helper: A Systematic Approach to Effective Helping*, Brooks/Cole 1986.
2. See, for example, Bill Kirkpatrick, *AIDS: Sharing the Pain*, DLT 1988.
3. A study of titles in the SPCK New Library of Pastoral Care reveals failure to define pastoral theology in any rigorous manner. See also, P. H. Ballard, ed., *The Foundations of Pastoral Studies and Practical Theology*, University of Cardiff 1986.
4. This approach is explored in further depth in David Deeks, *Pastoral Theology, An Enquiry*, Epworth Press 1987 and in Michael Wilson, *A Coat of Many Colours: Pastoral Studies of the Christian Way of Life*, Epworth Press 1988.
5. See, for example, Paul Seighart, *AIDS and Human Rights: A UK Perspective*, British Medical Foundation for AIDS 1989.
6. The African situation is described by Dr Cecile de Sweemer, Co-ordinator of Health Services in Africa, in David Hallam, ed., *AIDS issues: Confronting the Challenges*, New York, Pilgrim Press, 1989.
7. See James Fowler, *Faith Development and Pastoral Care*, Fortress Press 1987.

1

To the Churches with Love
from the Lighthouse

Stephen Pattison

This chapter is a personal theological reflection on a meeting which took place in London in July 1989 between contributors to this book, people living closely with AIDS or HIV, and those concerned to provide care for them. I have written elsewhere on the nature of theological reflection. Suffice it to say that I see this activity as basically the process of critical conversation and interrogation between contemporary situations or experience, aspects of the Christian theological tradition, and insights from sources of contemporary knowledge, for example, the social sciences.[1]

I want to make it quite clear at the outset that I am conscious of the limitations of my own perceptions. The words which follow are based on my own insights gained from the meeting. They have not been agreed or examined by other participants who might have said very different things. On a different day, with different people in a different setting, my reflection might have gone in a completely different direction. I do not want to give the impression of spurious universality, objectivity, consensus or distance. I regard this as a disposable document recording first reactions, not as the foundation for future system. It can be treated as throw-away theology (lasting and authoritative insights take a long time to evolve), though I hope there is enough integrity and faithfulness to situation and tradition in it to make it worth reading.

One of the most important developments of the last century or so has been the realization that theology, or theologies, are human constructs which reflect the context, interests and biases of those who formulate and use them.[2] This means that I must tell you something of my background and known biases so that you can evaluate what I say later more accurately. It is still uncommon for theologians to make overt their personal origins, situations and beliefs in their public discourse. In the present context I believe it is a methodological prerequisite.

I am a 35-year-old white male of middle class origin and education. Having been brought up in Quakerism, I became a member of the Church of England, attracted by its sacramentalism, did a degree in Biblical Studies and completed training for the Anglican ministry in Scotland where I became fascinated by the relationship between belief and action in the subject area known as Practical Theology. After a brief curacy, I researched the relationship between liberation theology and pastoral care in mental illness hospitals. I was then a pastoral studies teacher in a theological college and subsequently a university lecturer in pastoral studies for five years.

My present work as secretary of a community health council springs from a long-lasting concern for social justice and from trying to ensure that belief is fleshed out in action. I married relatively young and am now divorced with no children. I have not married again. I believe myself to be predominantly heterosexual in sexual orientation. Like most of the population, I have lesbian and gay friends and relations. A number of my relatives have suffered severe mental illness. On their behalf as well as that of gay and divorced people, I have a fair sense of outrage against the indifference and rejection of the Churches at an institutional level. Naively perhaps, I believe the Church should do good to people, learn from them and build them up, not make people who are already having a bad time feel worse. I had already written to some extent in these terms, though less personally, in a previous publication on the judgement of AIDS.[3] However, before July 1989 when the meeting described and discussed below took place, I had never knowingly met anyone living closely with HIV or AIDS.

So to the Lighthouse. The Lighthouse, near Notting Hill in London, is a brand new imposing building which could contain smart offices. It houses some hospice beds for people living with AIDS, a home care hospice service and endless training teams, facilities and meeting rooms, as well as a very pleasant restaurant which is open to the public. In fact, the fifteen or so people who met in July 1989 did not meet in the Lighthouse but in a basement opposite, altogether less intimidating, but hot, sticky and dark on an overcast but very warm and humid day. The London Underground was recovering from industrial action. It was the worst kind of day to be meeting in the city, and even Birmingham, where I live, seemed an attractive alternative.

For about six hours, a changing population talked in a free-ranging way about issues relating to AIDS or HIV. We were male and female, gay and straight, married and unmarried, divorced, Christian, non-Christian, post-Christian. Some were writers, some academics, some care providers, some people living with HIV or AIDS. Most were over thirty and under seventy. All were white. Some had been or were ordained Christian ministers, most were not. After the inevitable but enjoyable introductions and discussion of expectations we settled into relaxed, honest and interesting conversation punctuated only by new arrivals and early departures. The frustrations of the London Underground soon seemed far away.

We talked about this book. What was it intended to do? Would it make the institutional Churches take action? Could it change the world or just encourage the struggling and help provide community for them amidst hostility? People talked about the importance of being listened to, about the need for good and truthful meanings, about being victims, about living creatively with HIV—and being destroyed by it. Personal stories began to emerge about what HIV had done to and for people, about responses from carers and professionals, about rejection by churches, their ministers and leaders, about hurtful decisions made in other places. The experiences of one person led to others expounding theirs. Emotional themes emerged: terror, isolation, togetherness, guilt, shame, acceptance, the importance of being honest with oneself and being understood. Spontaneously, naturally and unportentously, amidst all this, great existential themes also appeared: life, death, destruction, creation, fear, evil, chaos, spirituality, solitude and love. It is important to say that there seemed to be no experts, only explorers. Our conversation was an unfinished beginning and came to no conclusions or answers. So, where to begin a theological reflection on this all too brief, but rich, experience?

I think I must start with the experience itself. For all of us, being together was important. Within a very short time there was a profound sense that we were glad to be there with each other. We felt sustained, challenged, supported and accepted in a group of strangers sharing no past and no future. For me at any rate, the experience was fundamental not ephemeral. As individuals we were recognized and accepted. We went away with more than we brought because of the generosity of others' willing sharing and communication. It would have been possible for me to worship with this group and, in more unanimously 'Christian' circles, I would describe the meeting as a spiritual experience in the broadest and most worthwhile sense. A meeting around the topic of living and dying with HIV with a very mixed group of strangers produced an experience of solidarity, encounter, challenge and togetherness which I would want to call Church. It is this experience of Church which I now want to examine more closely and interrogate in relation to the institutional Churches.[4]

Perhaps it is no accident that I should begin to think of our meeting as embodying an experience of authentic Church. Some of the people in our group living directly with HIV themselves described their experience in terms directly analogous to being converted. First comes the experience of realizing that you are HIV positive. The familiar world is turned upside down. Suddenly life becomes both very precious and very precarious. It is important to live every second; everything from fear to hope is very vivid. It is not an exaggeration to say that some people felt they had really come to life for the first time at this fateful moment, a moment both unfair and wonderful. A complete reordering of priorities and horizons takes place in the wake of what might truly be called a baptism of fire.

Moving beyond initial 'conversion' to fulness of present life there are moments of doubt and terror. Isolation and uncertainty loom, there are periods of feeling well and feeling very ill. Fortunately, there is the possibility of community around the aweful reality of AIDS. There are fellow experiencers, and places like the Lighthouse and CARA (Care and Resources for People Affected by HIV/AIDS) witness to the importance of fellowship, support and self-help in the company of others who know the reality of the experience. Group meetings and friendships become important and deep.

There is an almost monastic spirituality and discipline surrounding the experience of HIV/AIDS for some people. Confession of feelings to groups is important, as are strict diets (to maintain physical fitness) and meditation/visualization exercises.[5] The aim is to survive and live as creatively as possible with the disease, to maintain some sense of control and self-esteem in the face of chaos and immense uncertainty.

The fact that we were meeting at all bears witness to an eagerness to evangelize. People were keen to speak of their experience, if not to convert others, at least to make them fully aware of how they felt and how their experiences had affected them. There was no sense that these things should be spoken of only in private and hidden from public view. People living closely with HIV rightly assert that the whole of society is living with AIDS (just as some Christians assert that we are all living with the present reality of salvation whether we like it or not). They are keen that society should realize its situation, take responsibility and learn from their experience. The idea that a 'sacred text' in the shape of this book might appear to convey experience to a wider audience was welcomed and applauded.

The people living closely with HIV/AIDS who met at the London Lighthouse (itself perhaps a sort of cathedral in this context!) were deeply alive and aware people converted to life by the threat of death, longing to share what they had with others in the context of compassionate fellowship, members of a new kind of spiritual movement or church. Yet nearly all of them, as well as other participants in the conversation, felt deeply alienated from the institutional Churches which they saw as unresponsive and rejecting. Stories were told of people being rejected by colleagues and superiors when HIV was diagnosed. Those who had no close relationship with the institutional Churches in adult life seemed to feel they had nothing to offer except reinforcement of guilt, shame and rejection, emotions which denied and diminished at a time when positive self-image and acceptance are vital. It seemed that many felt they had discovered that the reconciliation, love, acceptance and forgiveness they had sought all their lives had been obtained only through the 'secular' spiritualities, groups and relationships which have sprung up around AIDS. For some, there was anger against the institutional Churches for not living up to their high ideals and showing appropriate care. Others had never expected Churches to provide that care or attention anyway.

Personally, I do not find a need to lament the fact that people find love, care and reconciliation outside the Churches. But it worries and perplexes me greatly that organizations which are founded round a life and a death seem unable to cope with life and death when they present themselves in people living closely with HIV/AIDS. These people offer their own vision of fulness of life and community in the face of the terror and isolation of death. If the Churches cannot perceive and receive this, something has gone wrong. The experience of people living closely with AIDS is one of life, love, reconciliation and community alongside isolation, fear and destruction. It summons the institutional Church to come forth from its sepulchre and to discover the content rather than the form of resurrection in relation to life and death. If it cannot do so, the loss will be its own. Will the Churches accept and recognize the gift of life or will they cling to death, even 'if someone should rise from the dead' (cf. Luke 16.31)?

In her book *Purity and Danger*, the social anthropologist Mary Douglas writes,

> Granted that disorder spoils pattern; it also provides the materials of pattern. Order implies restriction; from all possible materials, a limited selection has been made and from all possible relations a limited set has been used. So disorder by implication is unlimited, no pattern has been realised in it, but its potential for patterning is indefinite. This is why, though we seek to create order, we do not simply condemn disorder. We recognise that it is destructive to existing patterns; also that it has potentiality. *It symbolises both danger and power*.[6]

One of the main functions of any religion is to cope with chaos and disorder: to tame it and make ordered existence possible. Ironically, however, the continuing life of any religion depends on its ability to be able to tap the energy or power emerging from chaos. Thus, within the

Judaeo-Christian tradition, religion has been energized by being disrupted by new inbreakings of chaos or Spirit in, for example, the ministries of prophets or Jesus. Spirit is profoundly ambiguous; it appears to have organizing and controlling features (cf. Genesis 1 where Spirit orders latent matter), but also disruptive and disordering aspects (cf. Mark 1.12 where the Spirit literally throws the newly baptized Jesus out into the desert).

Christianity depends for its very existence on keeping in touch with the energy and resource of chaos at the margins. Ultimately, this chaos is most powerfully represented in the annihilation promised by death. The world is more disordered and disintegrated than we can possibly imagine or cope with. In the end it destroys our bodies, lives and meanings.[7] Hence the power of a religion which places resurrection at its centre.

Christianity offers the possibility of some kind of overcoming of chaos and creation of meaning, relationship, purpose and community. But it can do this only if it remains in contact with the turbulent forces of life and death which it seeks to control. Inevitably, over time, religions tend to fossilize and routinize themselves, to pretend that there is in fact no chaos at all, only order and tranquillity. At this point, they become anaesthetized and start to die. In their death throes they resist the forces of life and death ever more vigorously. In doing so they minimize the fear of death but lose the possibility of life. Individuals and communities who are full of life or genuinely face death are a threat to chaos, and death-avoiding institutions. They are rejected.

Ironically, they also offer such institutions the only hope they have for continuing life. Life comes from the margins where life and death mingle and break into the world of meaning and pattern.[8] Small wonder, then, that institutional Churches have little place for those who have undergone the terrible baptism into living with HIV. Recognizing this perennial tendency, Karl Barth once described religion as humanity's last protest against God, and directed the attention of religious people again and again to the living and disturbing chaotic word of the gospel which must be refracted through the life of the community which calls itself Church.[9]

Contemporary Churches at a structural, institutional level fear the forces of life and death and endeavour to flee from them. They are in good company, for the original disciples of Jesus reacted in much the same way when they witnessed the inbreaking mighty works of God in his ministry. New life can be as disruptive and unwelcome as sudden death. At the tomb on Easter morning the disciples were afraid to find it empty, not delighted (Mark 16.8). Fear and awe are authentic aspects of religious experience. By definition, they never become less fearful or awesome, though the memory of them may be domesticated, routinized and institutionalized. Later I will discuss the importance of re-siting the fear and chaos excited by living with AIDS within the Christian belief in resurrection. First, however, I want to discuss the structural and attitudinal aspects of institutionalized church life which complement and buttress the rejection of life and death intruding at the margins of domesticated religion.

Criticism of the institutional structures of the Church, implied or overt, must be as nearly as old as the Church itself. Some contemporary critiques, however, raise new questions in very sharp ways. Don Cupitt argues that the Church is a power structure which is based to some extent on coercion. The politics of subjection based on a hierarchical dualism which is ultimately based on sexism holds sway.[10] Patriarchal rationalism, complemented by pyramidal rank-orders and authority, are important features of Churches which are becoming increasingly narrow and defensive in a post-modern world.

As the Churches find themselves more and more marginalized from contemporary life they reject the inbreaking of critical thought and become 'philistine and morally vicious'.[11] Orthodoxy and monolithic concepts of truth and reality are commended together with public rationality, objective truth and univocal meaning to provide 'tools of domination'. Implicitly, these are monarchical ideas: 'one God, one Truth, one chain of command'.[12] Modes of operation are non-rational, authoritarian and populist. Right from the beginning, the Church has been 'a punitive power structure with an orthodoxy'.[13] Church members internalize the norms of the system and oppress and repress themselves and others. Pluralism and variety are feared above all things. Cupitt sets out the conflict between the institutional power religion which Christianity was to become over against the more charismatic and open faith available to Paul in a series of contrasting pairs: Institution—Charisma; The Church—The Spirit; Doctrine—Mysticism; Order—Freedom; Law—Gospel; Obedience—Expression; Hierarchy—Equality; An objective, public authority-system—The authority principle internalized.[14]

Cupitt's critique is amplified by that of Graham Shaw who points up the reluctance of the Church to acknowledge a shadow side to its existence.[15] Although the Church is founded round a fundamental message of freedom and forgiveness, this has frequently been suppressed to buttress social power and control. Christianity has been authoritarian, oppressive and divisive to secure its own position and significance. It has sought the illusion of permanence, been intolerant of criticism, rejected disturbing experiences from without and suffered from the delusion that it is good and perfect at the expense of having to create groups of 'enemies' outside to embody that which is feared and hated. Shaw speaks with feeling of the 'cost of authority'.

One does not have to assent to all these points individually to acknowledge their cumulative force. Together, they present a picture of a Church which in many ways is bound to reject strangers and those from 'outside'. This Church is 'totalized' in that it resists and resents any perspective other than its own. Such a Church values the past rather than the present, rules rather than relationships, orthodoxy rather than pluralism, structures rather than people, male rather than female, mind rather than body, stability rather than change, barriers rather than communication, distance rather than intimacy, exclusivity rather than inclusiveness, dualism rather than holism, power rather than vulnerability, command rather than mutuality, passivity rather than activity, reaction rather than initiative, hierarchical leadership rather than equality, the strong voices at the centre rather than the weaker ones at the edges. It maintains a sense of its own goodness and power by designating 'out-groups' who embody badness and are made to feel impotent. It evangelizes by endlessly talking and pronouncing rather than by acting and listening. Its acceptance is utterly conditional; if people will turn themselves into passive victims and convert themselves to receive the ministrations of the Church gratefully, they can be saved, especially if they seem suitably ashamed of their former lives. It has no capacity to learn or receive graciously from those who live and die on its margins or outside it.

In fact, the existence of those who dwell in the shadow of the chaos of death yet are manifestly alive, refusing to behave as passive victims to be treated as objects of compassion, is simply infuriating to the institutionalized Church. It challenges its sense of meaning, goodness, power and control. The 'dying' should passively ebb away into a tranquil eternity, not dance on the lids of their tombs, reject the cheap compassion of the Church and start giving it lessons about life, love and community in the present. The vision of a person fully alive, especially if regarded as immoral and sinful by virtue of sexual orientation or behaviour, walking around, accepting themselves and others, being angry and assertive, is a deeply threatening and inconvenient one. It is such a vision which some people living closely with AIDS present.

In practical terms, the problem presented to the Churches by people living closely with HIV/AIDS is one of prejudice. Sociologists have clearly set out the processes whereby some groups and individuals come to be recognized as stigmatized and unacceptable due to their occupancy of negatively sanctioned social roles. This is all part of defining norms for social order. Ill people of all kinds can feel themselves to be stigmatized and rejected. Gay people living with AIDS suffer from a double dose of stigmatization, for they not only deviate from norms of health and are seen as a health 'threat', but also threaten sexual norms.[16] The latter falls almost in the realm of unforgivable sin for the institutional Churches, at least on a public level; for sexuality, too, represents the reality of anarchy, potential disorder and chaos. Christianity has never really decided whether it likes bodily sexuality or not. In the absence of a positive theology of incarnational sex, it has decided to control it largely by condemnation. Divorced and remarried people can bear witness to this as eloquently as gays.[17]

The mirror image of the stigmatization and rejection experienced by people living closely with AIDS (and let it be recalled that not all of them are gay, though if they are not they enjoy the guilt by association or 'courtesy stigma' which contrives to make the whole area appear to the general public as a Stygian swamp of immorality and disease) is the prejudice latent within the institutional Churches.[18] Prejudice is 'a predisposition towards people which is not derived from adequate information'.[19] Some of its most salient features in the present context are as follows. First, it is based on dualistic thinking and a ranking of pairs so that one part is good, the other bad; thus, heterosexual and homosexual are distinguished (dualism) and the former is held to be 'good' while the latter is regarded as 'bad' (hierarchical distinction).

Prejudices reflect a desire to control the uncertainties of life and they enhance the sense of control and self-esteem of those who are prejudiced. Buttressed by adaptable sterotypes ('all gays are evil and immoral'), they attain stability through irrational psychodynamics and both reflect and reinforce current distributions of social power.[20] A Church which is losing social significance and influence in wider society while having to cope with great uncertainty will find it attractive and easy to cope with this loss and to retain self-esteem and control by stereotyping socially stigmatized and less significant groups like gays or mentally ill people. The cost of relinquishing such prejudice appears to be disintegration, loss of control, chaos. The price of acceptance and understanding is then very high.

An important theological motif to pick up in relation to prejudice in the Church is that of crucifixion. Rather than seeking to bolster his self-esteem and control over chaos and people, attitudes which lie at the centre of prejudice, Jesus surrendered those things in dying on a cross outside a city wall, rejected by his own people. The institutional Churches will always have enormous difficulty in following the example of giving up self-esteem, righteousness, and life for the sake of others. Happily, it is not a challenge they can ever avoid entirely, for it lies at the heart of their tradition, However, the motif of resurrection seems important too, particularly in the perspective of our conversations at the Lighthouse.

The problem is that the institutional Churches have preserved a tradition but lost a memory. Christianity began with a person who lived life fully, even in the face of death. The doctrine of the resurrection, whose form is so lovingly cherished by some Christians even as it is stretched out like barbed wire to exclude fellow human beings from the Church, embodies the possibility of life, fellowship and love in the face of death and chaos. Christianity is as it is because it preserves within it liberating memories about life in the face of death. Rather than being used to distance people, fend them off and exclude them, it could be rediscovered as a rallying point for fellowship and community in the face of the annihilating chaos which surrounds us all. There is no answer to the reality of death. The life and community of people living with AIDS suggests, however, that there is the possibility of enlivening relationship in the face of it. We cannot accompany one another beyond the moment of death. But the subversive memory of life in death suggests that we can learn and live together up to that point, refusing to relinquish hold of one another and so wresting some kind of new life from the living void from which we sprang and to which we all return.

'Lazarus, come forth' (John 11.43). These words have been ringing in my head as I have written. It is, of course, very dubious to quote nuggets of congenial Scripture completely out of context to amplify and give authority to one's point of view. Nonetheless, these words, which come from the story of the raising of Lazarus in John's Gospel, embody the reflections from the Lighthouse which I now share with the Church. People living with HIV and AIDS are a positive part of our body corporate. They have much to teach the Churches about life in the face of death. The fact that this is not an original conclusion does not diminish its significance. We need to be able to hear and receive them. If we do not, the loss will be ours. We must find ways of sharing, celebrating and protesting against the realities of life and death which belong to us all in the name of Jesus the risen and living one. If this means radical restructuring of treasured beliefs, attitudes and structures, so be it. The real fellowship and compassion experienced at an individual level amongst some Christians and people living closely with HIV must no longer be contradicted by the heavy-handed death-dealing prejudices of the institutionalized Church.[21]

NOTES

1. For theological reflection see S. Pattison, 'Some straw for the bricks: a basic introduction to theological reflection', *Contact* 99, 1989; M. H. Taylor, *Learning to Care*, SPCK 1983.
2. The theologians of liberation make this more clear than anyone. See further, e.g. J. L. Segundo, *The Liberation of Theology*, Dublin, Gill & Macmillan, 1977.
3. S. Pattison, *Alive and Kicking: Towards a Practical Theology of Illness and Healing*, SCM 1989.
4. I am reminded of Ruether's words here: 'The Church is where the good news of liberation from sexism is preached, where the Spirit is present to empower us to renounce patriarchy, where a community committed to the new life of mutuality is gathered together and nurtured, and where the community is spreading this vision and struggle to others', see R. R. Ruether, *Sexism and God Talk: Towards a Feminist Theology* (SCM 1983), p. 213.
5. Some sense of this almost religious routine can be gained from C. Saunders, 'Living positively', *New Statesman and Society* (27 January 1989), pp. 13-16.
6. M. Douglas, *Purity and Danger* (Routledge & Kegan Paul 1966), p. 94. My emphasis.
7. 'Death is the axis around which every religious system revolves, the axis around which it is completely organised' J. Pohier, *God in Fragments* (SCM 1985), p. 99. See also D. Rowe, *The Construction of Life and Death*, Fontana 1989.
8. cf. E. Dussel, *Ethics and the Theology of Liberation*, Maryknoll, NY, Orbis, 1978. Dussel eloquently argues that liberating change can only come from the margins of society where people have no vested interest in the established 'totalized' order and sb are open to the possibility of new things occurring.
9. I have not been able to trace this quotation, but trust that I have made the right attribution here. Whether or not Barth made this assertion, I believe it remains a valid one in its own right in the present context.
10. D. Cupitt, *Radicals and the Future of the Church*, SCM 1989. The notion of 'hierarchical dualism' comes from D. Shields, *Growing Beyond Prejudices*, Mystic, Conn., Twenty-Third Publications, 1986.
11. Cupitt, *Radicals and the Future of the Church*, p. 9.
12. ibid., p. 14.
13. ibid., p. 17.
14. D. Cupitt, *The New Christian Ethics* (SCM 1988), p. 71.
15. G. Shaw, *The Cost of Authority*, SCM 1983. See J. Sanford, *Evil: The Shadow Side of Reality*, New York, Crossroad, 1981; A. Belford Ulanov, *The Wisdom of the Psyche*, Cambridge, Mass., Cowley, 1988, for more on the way in which Christianity ignores the 'evil and bad' side of reality to concentrate one-sidedly on the 'positive and virtuous' aspects of existence.
16. For more on stigmatization see Pattison, *Alive and Kicking*, ch. 5. Spong writes, 'Behind prejudice there is also fear. We reject that which we cannot manage. We condemn what we do not understand. We set up a means of control to render powerless those dynamic realities we know to be powerful. No aspect of our humanity is invested with more anxieties, yearnings, emotions and needs than is our sexual nature. So sex is a major arena in which the prejudice of human beings finds expression' J. S. Spong, *Living in Sin?*, (San Francisco, Harper & Row, 1988), p. 23.
17. Unfortunately, stigmatized people internalize their own stigma and treat themselves and each other as 'problems'. This accounts for the fact that many people who perceive themselves to be 'bad' leave the Churches. This ensures that the Churches have no problem people around. They become invisible or go away—a very subtle mechanism for maintaining a sense of institutional goodness but one which ensures distance, double standards and deceit in pastoral care.
18. See E. Goffman, *Stigma*, Penguin 1968.
19. Shields, *Growing Beyond Prejudice*, p. 2.

20. cf. Shields, pp. x-xi, for these points.
21. Pastoral care badly needs to be delivered from the double standards which decree that people in general can be condemned from the pulpit while as individuals in private they are treated with understanding and compassion. The lack of integrity here undermines the credibility and accessibility of the Church. It is no way to cope with the gaps between ethics and pastoral care, love and justice, ideal and reality, and is deeply insidious. It produces the kind of thinking which finds expression in 'love the sinner, hate the sin' attitudes prevalent in the Churches. Actually, people do not want to be loved despite what they are, but because of what they are. Anything else is not love! See further J. Nelson, *Embodiment*, SPCK 1979; S. Pattison, *A Critique of Pastoral Care*, SCM 1988.

Nigel Sheldrick

Nigel discovered he had the HIV virus in 1985. He developed Karposi sarcoma in the latter part of 1987 which resulted in lesions disfiguring his body. Despite being unable to work for two years, he continued to live enthusiastically and creatively for life. This account of his experiences was written shortly before his death in January 1990.

Somebody recently said, and I agree, that people with HIV fall broadly into two categories. First there are those who become hopeless, who feel themselves to be a victim of AIDS. The second category are those who somehow use it and are able to speak optimistically and positively about it. I have had to work hard to live with the tension and paradox between these two experiences. It has been a fascinating journey—a gift in that it has helped me to support and be supported by others in the same situation, and helped me to look at my own feelings, my hurts and pains.

Of course, there have been hard times. I have gone through a lot of loneliness and despair and anger and grief of all sorts. But I know and have experienced that when I get rid of all the emotional rubbish and my anger, when I am able to shout, 'Oh my God, this is awful, I have been abandoned and I am on my own', then fear subsides and faith and hope emerge. For me the opposite of hope is fear and when I have gone through utter despair and lost even hope, it is like entering a new doorway; faith emerges out of my discharging anger and fear and I have sensed a tremendous feeling that everything is all right in the universe. I remember once after a hard workshop I came out of my loneliness and despair and experienced the most inspirational ten days of my life. I felt a sense of connectedness with people and the world. I sensed that life was chaotic yet beautiful. I felt like singing and dancing. I felt like going up to people and grabbing them and saying, 'You are wonderful, you really are bloody wonderful.' I wanted to say to them all that your pain and hardships are good; embrace it and experience it and you can change it.

I have a tremendous sense that God is alongside me in this experience. It's not always easy to perceive God's presence, there have been times when I was in utter despair and God was just absent. Even though I had the support around me I was going through a period of feeling very alone with it. Somehow I found myself saying that I know what Jesus meant about suffering and how it was like a very sacred thing. I was alone and crying but paradoxically felt that it was fine, that this was how it should be. And so maybe, we have to go through feelings of utter desperation and loneliness and desolation to really fully experience what it might mean to have God alongside. We can know something intellectually but it is a different matter altogether actually to feel it. I feel grateful that through my journey into my despair and anger and hopelessness I have become aware, I have been released into a sense of the massive potential of life. It seems to me that this is the essence of everything—our potential for everything amidst nothing. It's a paradox that I have to live and relive as I try to uncover what AIDS means for me.

I feel at the moment that, just possibly, physical death is a doorway to all of us realizing that incredible spontaneity and potential that is continually bursting around and in us. Perhaps heaven and hell are sort of within us and we have the potential to live in heaven now—if we can go through the veil of anguish and tears that we have built up over the years. If only we could really see our splendour, if only we could all see each other's splendour what a different world it would be. My dream is that we can all put our own vision of life into practice every day.

So, I regard myself as on a journey with trials and tribulations, with darkest despair and also hope, laughter and happiness. My hope is that those around can sit with me, be alongside me as I struggle and grow.

2

AIDS, Shame and Suffering

Grace Jantzen

A man with AIDS wrote,

> At the age of 28 I wake up every morning to face the very real possibility of my own death.
>
> Whenever I am asked by members of the media or by curious healthy people what we talk about in our group I am struck by the intractable gulf that exists between the sick and the well: what we talk about is survival.
>
> Mostly we talk about what it feels like to be treated like lepers who are treated as if they are morally, if not literally, contagious.[1]

People with AIDS and HIV are the lepers of modern society. They are looked upon with horror, revulsion and fear. There is fear about any form of contact, from eating together to sharing a communion cup to offering an embrace or a kiss of peace and welcome. Like the lepers in medieval times, people with AIDS and HIV face not only physical revulsion but also moral disapproval, the attitude that their condition is a punishment for sin or that they have brought it upon themselves through sexual activity or drug use that is feared and condemned by the majority. Their human dignity is undervalued and undermined, not least by the Church.

Yet the Church has had better examples of how lepers should be treated, and it is worth considering one such example as we try to come to a more Christian response to AIDS. According to his biographers, Francis of Assisi was a fastidious young man. He was horrified by poverty and by all forms of suffering, but nothing raised his revulsion so much as leprosy. If he chanced to see a leper while he was out riding, he would dismount, hold his nose, and send a messenger to give some alms. Then one day, at the beginning of his conversion, he came unexpectedly upon a leper on the road. His first impulse was to recoil: then he remembered his desire for discipleship.

> He slipped off his horse and ran to kiss the man. When the leper put out his hand as if to receive some alms, Francis gave him money and a kiss.[2]

This was for Francis a significant turning point in his understanding of Christ. Now that he had identified himself with Christ and with the lepers, in action and not merely in theory, his practical understanding of the incarnation deepened in direct proportion to his active obedience.

> From that time on he clothed himself with a spirit of poverty, a sense of humility and a feeling of intimate devotion. Formerly he used to be horrified not only by close dealing with lepers but by their very sight, even from a distance; but now he rendered humble service to the lepers with human concern and devoted kindness . . . because of Christ crucified, who according to the text of the prophet was despised *as a leper*. He visited their houses frequently, generously distributed alms to them, and with great compassion kissed their hands and their mouths.[3]

It is clear that his biographers do not see this connection as accidental. It was as Francis responded to the invitation to follow Christ in his identification with the lepers that his spiritual vision was enlarged: his love for Christ increased in direct relation to his involvement with the outcasts of his society. Nor do his biographers intend us to see this increased understanding and love as a sort of divine reward for heroic behaviour. Rather, it is because Christ really is the one who made himself one with the outcasts that he can be found in solidarity with them. The lepers constituted a concrete opportunity to learn to know and love Christ.[4]

I wish to suggest that as the lepers for St Francis, so people today with AIDS and HIV offer us the opportunity to rediscover Christ. I am not saying that the Church is being offered an opportunity for condescending charity or alms to 'victims' while we keep well out of the way and metaphorically hold our noses. I am not even saying only that the AIDS crisis offers the possibility for genuine service, though it certainly does. I am making the much stronger claim that for all the human tragedy of AIDS, like the human tragedy of leprosy, it is also an opportunity to reopen ourselves to people who have the virus, to their love and dignity as well as their suffering and fear, their sexuality and mortality—in short, their humanity—*and our own*. And if the incarnation is about the solidarity of God with humankind, then practical identification with people with AIDS can send us back to reading the New Testament with joyous insight that we didn't have before.

One of the avenues along which we may grow together in a deeper openness to incarnation is by exploring the revulsion and shame associated with AIDS and HIV. Like St Francis cringing with revulsion from the lepers, our first reaction is often to cringe from those with AIDS. Now, although we need to explore what we do with that revulsion, I would suggest that we should not be too hard on ourselves for having it in the first place. It is an entirely human reaction to recoil from the sight of disease, deformity or pain, or even from the awareness of serious illness where no symptoms are apparent. We are horrified by these things, and we should be. They are horrific. They are not to be romanticized or sentimentalized; and our revulsion to them should not be suppressed, lest we develop calluses around our souls.

Furthermore, encounter with serious disease is a reminder of our own mortality. Again, it would be inhuman not to cringe from death. It may be that we can face it and come to terms with it, but to be unmoved by it is subhuman, not superhuman. When we face our own mortality in the body of another it is right to be appalled, for their sake and our own. The question is not whether we feel fear and revulsion but what we do with it. I have suggested that what we must *not* do is deny those feelings, pretend they are not there, refuse to let the symptoms and suffering of fellow human beings bother us, or repress our fear at their mortality and ours.

Another common way of coping with our feelings of horror is to offer compassion at a distance, as St Francis did, keeping our own noses carefully covered while sending charity, perhaps very generous charity, by way of a messenger or go-between, but avoiding contact at all costs, lest somehow we be polluted. But what does this accomplish? The recipients of the charity, while perhaps having to accept it out of their necessity, are diminished in their humanity by it, forced to receive condescension, to accept the role of victim. They have to see themselves as people whom no one wishes to touch, people who cause revulsion, people who cannot be received and loved. When one is already suffering and fearful, the burden of such rejection is intolerable. As for us as givers of such charity, we are isolated not only from those who suffer but from our own humanity as well by such refusal to encounter disease and death. We refuse ourselves the opportunity to come to terms with them, and by keeping our distance from those who suffer, distance ourselves also from learning about the dignity and courage, humour and hope available to those who use their illness to discover their meaning and their worth. We deprive ourselves of truth and of love. We deprive ourselves also of God, for God sits with the sufferer against whom we hold our nose.

A further way in which we deal with our feelings of revulsion, especially if we are theologians, is to construct a theory about suffering. Suffering is horrifying: surely a compassionate God must be as horrified as we are? Why then does God continue to permit such suffering, when surely it is within the competence of omnipotence to intervene? These are genuine questions, and it is right that we should ponder deeply the nature of God in the face of suffering. But what can too easily happen is that as we seek for answers to our concerns we turn the whole thing into an intellectual exercise, offering explanation and counter-explanation, theodicy and counter-theodicy, until what may have begun as an effort at understanding human suffering ends as an insulation against it.[5]

Particularly insidious is the sort of theodicy which is so intent on preserving God from all responsibility for suffering that it attributes the responsibility to the sufferer. In some contexts the so-called 'free will defence', the theory that all suffering is to be attributed to the free choices of moral agents, reads like a classic exercise in blaming the victim. It is a syndrome only too well known in cases of rape and violence against women: somehow the victim must have asked for it, must be at fault. And it is applied with particular venom to people with HIV and AIDS: they must be deserving of illness because of their sexual practices or drug use or even, in the case of African and Caribbean people with AIDS, because of the race to which they belong. The natural physical revulsion that we feel about suffering and death is turned into a moral revulsion, an imputation to the sufferer of moral failure for which they are being justly punished. By such a strategy it is possible to preserve both our own righteousness and God's, setting ourselves up as with divine authority against the ones 'contaminated' through their own fault.

Other essays in this book show how utterly misguided such an attitude is, and I will not repeat their discussion of it. What I wish to do, however, is to draw attention to the connection between fear and blame that is apparent in such a stance. As already noted, we are all afraid of suffering and death; we are also afraid of the unknown and the marginal. Now for many of us sexuality represents something that is deeply unknown and problematical. That is of course not to say that we are not sexually active; but for many of us our sexual impulses and involvements are more complicated than we like to admit. Our society is strongly heterosexist; that is, it sees heterosexuality as the biological and moral norm. In such a society there is an enormous investment in denying, even to ourselves, any homosexual feelings or relationships, and refusing to acknowledge that part of ourselves which is drawn to the same sex. This is true even though it has been widely known for some time that most people are in fact drawn to both sexes to a greater or lesser degree.

Now although AIDS and HIV are by no means restricted to homosexuals, they are popularly so associated in the public mind. This means that when we confront a person with AIDS we are confronted not only by our revulsion at sickness and death but also by our ambivalent sexuality. Many of us find this—especially the combination —deeply threatening. If within ourselves there is repressed discomfort about homosexuality, AIDS is available to become a focus for our fear and uncertainty. As Seymour Kleinberg has said,

> Since the late sixties we have all been living in a society at war, mostly with itself, under dire stress, and the sexual behaviour of gay men has become the radical exponent of tension and disaffection widespread in all adult life. We have come to symbolize every confusion about sexuality in modern history, and thus, we are objects of fascination and abhorrence.[6]

Our societal anxieties emerge as anger against homosexuals, and blame heaped upon those who have AIDS and HIV. The Church has much to answer for in this, both in its frequent eagerness to be the ringleader of the stone-throwing brigade, and, more fundamentally, in its failure to develop a theology of sexuality. It is deeply ironic that a religion named after one who was incarnate love should have so total a vacuum in its theology of embodied desire, and be so frightened of public discourse about sexuality.

For people who have contracted HIV or AIDS, the effect of all this is invidious, leading all too easily to an internalization of the shame and revulsion which society projects on to them, and eroding their sense of self-worth. Anyone who has a serious illness which may generate painful or difficult to manage symptoms is already confronted with bewilderment about her body, fear, physical and mental pain, anger, and often revulsion at the abhorrent symptoms. She may also have to confront not only her own fear and grief but also that of her friends and family as they try to cope with their own reactions, and with a certain level of stigmatization from society. As Dennis Altman has pointed out,

> to be stigmatized because of illness is hardly confined to people with AIDS: anyone suspected of carrying a disease will experience stigma, and it is a stigma that often extends to non-contagious diseases such as cancer and schizophrenia.[7]

But in the case of an illness like cancer, the attitude of society and Church is generally sympathetic and supportive: people consider it important to overcome such fear and revulsion as they might feel. Messages of love and encouragement pour in from family, friends and colleagues; at times when morale is low it is possible to ask for support and be confident that such a request will find a sympathetic response. This cannot take away the pain or the fear or even the sense of isolation in the face of possible death, but it does assure the ill person of her worth to those who love her, and of all the care and comfort they can give. It is very common for a person with a life-threatening illness to have periods of anguished questioning: Why me? What have I done to deserve this? But in the case of an illness like cancer it is possible to express such doubt and confusion to a friend or to a visiting minister and to receive assurances that the illness has nothing to do with sin, let alone with God's punishment: that these are natural and normal questions but that they are expressions of understandable rage and bewilderment, not signs that the ill person is particularly sinful or perverse.

People with AIDS and HIV ask these questions too. But because of the fear and suspicion and blame in society and in the Church toward drug use and homosexuality it is by no means a foregone conclusion that they will be offered the care and moral support that someone with some other life-threatening illness can count on. If a person with AIDS asks the vicar, 'Why me? What have I done to deserve this?', she or he may well get, not comfort, but a list of accusations probably coupled with an invitation to repent. At a time when vulnerability is highest and morale is lowest, self-esteem is further eroded by the opprobrium heaped upon them even by well-meaning individuals, let alone by attitudes of society percolated through the media. A person who is ill and frightened needs a lot of hugs: who will hug a person with AIDS?[8]

Even at the level of medical care major differences can arise. A person with cancer can rest assured of skilled and sympathetic medical attention, and does not need to add to her fears and grief about death any worry about whether appropriate funeral arrangements can be made. But for a person with AIDS it is always possible that some of the medical staff will be hostile; and there are still many undertakers who refuse their services. As well as the anxiety which such attitudes generate for the person with AIDS, there is inevitably a strong reinforcement of self-revulsion and shame.

By no means all people with AIDS and HIV are homosexual, but for those who are, such undermining of self-worth strikes at a very vulnerable point. All of us who are lesbian or gay have had the task of coming to terms with our sexuality in an oppressively heterosexist society, and for many of us it has not been easy. If we are Christians it has probably been more painful rather than less, as the Church has reinforced the attitude that respectability is to be accorded only to heterosexual marriages or to total celibacy. We have all been aware of how our families and friends and colleagues would prefer us to keep silent: as long as we do not confront them with the fact of our homosexual choices they will pretend that we are 'normal' and accord us respectability.

Yet we know too that respectability based on silence and pretence is bought at the expense of our self-esteem. Of course our sexuality is not the only or even necessarily the most important thing about us, any more than skin colour is the only or even the most important thing about blacks; but if this is the focus of denigrating attitudes, whether sexist or racist, then it must be affirmed with pride over and over again, partly to do what we can to change such attitudes, and partly to keep ourselves from colluding with the silence that offers respectability at the price of betrayal of a fundamental aspect of our identity. If this is hard for a person in a heterosexual marriage to understand, they might try to imagine what it would be like for them if they were placed in a situation where they could be accepted and esteemed only if they pretended that their spouse and children did not exist, or that their relationship with them was only casual.

For many of us, the decision to be open about being lesbian or gay has been costly even while also being enormously liberating and joyful. Attitudes of the unacceptability of homosexuality have been so internalized that even though we have begun to find our voice and our dignity and our pride it does not take much to tip us back into feeling vulnerable and insecure, uncertain of our value. Self-questioning and shame are easily induced.[9]

Accordingly, when a homosexual person contracts AIDS or HIV, and is faced with the revulsion and opprobrium of society and the Church, how can they help but find in themselves feelings of shame and guilt about their sexuality? How can they *not* feel angry with themselves and their lovers, horrified at what is happening, as if they are to blame and are being punished not only for their acts but for their very being? How can anyone not in their position begin to grasp the level of courage required to face their illness with dignity and without self-loathing?

When we try, however inadequately, to imagine ourselves in their position we can see how enormously important it is that the Church should be able to offer resources of dignity and support, not attitudes of shame. Like St Francis, the Church needs to stop holding its holy nose and take the men and women with AIDS and HIV into its arms and learn from them to see Christ. If the Gospels are about anything, they are about God coming alongside us, not identifying with the self-righteous, but giving dignity and esteem and support to those who were the outcasts of society by eating and drinking with them, touching them, being their friend. One thing that Jesus did not do was to reinforce internalized shame: what he did was to set people free to see their worth in his eyes and in God's.

In a Psalm which the Church has regularly taken as descriptive of

Christ, one of the qualities calling forth awe is his readiness to be alongside a sufferer:

> For he has not despised or abhorred the affliction of the
>   afflicted;
> and he has not hid his face from him,
>   but has heard, when he cried to him.
>
> (Psalm 22.24 RSV)

The Hebrew word translated 'abhorred' is *shiqef*: it means 'to shrink from, to detest or abominate'. It is used of the loathing that someone might have for filth, or for the detestation for idols that was to be engendered in the Israelites.[10] Such abhorrence would have been as familiar to those with leprosy in Jesus' time as it is to people with AIDS today: people would shrink from them, seeing them as filth and probably as wicked, coupling their fear and revulsion with moral rectitude.

We need to hear it plainly: *such an attitude is not God's attitude.* It is not God's attitude even if it is widely held in society. It is not God's attitude even if it is held by many who profess to speak in God's name. In Jesus we are shown that God does not detest or shrink from the affliction of the afflicted, but comes alongside in tenderness and brotherhood.

Such coming alongside is enormously important for the recovery of dignity. As Arnold Isenberg has pointed out, shame can only be healed by replacing it with self-worth. Such healing is to be contrasted with two inadequate efforts to deal with shame. The first of these is 'forgetfulness': that is, trying to pretend that the cause of shame is not there by thinking about other things, while still leaving intact the external and internal value judgements on which the feelings of shame feed. The other is 'consolation', in which the shame is not forgotten, but substitutes or compensations are suggested as though somehow if there are other good things about the person then the shameful things don't matter. Neither of these really resolves the shame; they only push it away, making it even harder to deal with. The only way in which it can be resolved is not by resorting to either pretence or substitutes, but by confronting the value judgement from which the shame originates.[11]

This is precisely what Jesus did. The society of his time shrank from and abhorred its outcasts, seeing them as sinners punished by God. Jesus counted them his friends, ate meals with them, spent time with them, thus reversing the value judgement that they were not of worth. It is also what St Francis did. He overcame his revulsion and his condescending charity by embracing the lepers, facing his own initial value judgement with the human reality of the sufferer. It is important to notice that he did not stop feeling revulsion first and then went and embraced the leper. He went and embraced the leper, and the love that he gave and received melted the revulsion away.

And this is what Christians are invited to do in response to people with AIDS and HIV. We need to confront our own value judgements which generate shame and fear with the loving acceptance of Christ. If we open ourselves to love people with AIDS and to receive love from them we will find that we can let go of our projections of shame and revulsion. As we spend time together we can find our attitudes being healed and our being alongside one another opening us to the presence of Christ. We may be challenged to be more in touch with our own sexuality and our mortality by women and men who have much to teach us about both. Who knows, we may even lose some of our self-righteousness!

Yet it would not be true to say that Jesus never expresses shame of anyone. In the Gospel of Mark there is a poignant sequence of events. Jesus performs miracles, multiplies loaves and fishes, heals a blind man. Then he asks his disciples who they say that he is, and Peter answers, 'You are the Christ'. But when he begins to teach them what that means, how being Christ means being on behalf of those who are seen as sinners and accepting the consequence of the cross and its shame, the disciples cannot handle it at all: Peter begins to rebuke him. The disciples wanted a Christ of power and invulnerability; Jesus offered them a totally different perspective. He taught them (and us) something about what following him means: it means taking up one's cross, doing in our own lives what Jesus did in his, giving our love and if necessary our reputations and our lives in being alongside those who suffer, just as Jesus was alongside them. And as Jesus concluded this teaching, for the only time in the Gospels Jesus speaks of shame: not shame at a sinner or a sufferer or an outcast, but shame at the pretended followers of his who disown the cross and the solidarity with human shame and suffering it represents.

> For whoever is ashamed of me and of my words . . . of them will the Son of man also be ashamed, when he comes in the glory of his Father with the holy angels.
>
> (Mark 8.38; parallel Luke 9.26)

Jesus projects no shame on those who suffer, not even when by the standards of his society they are sinful. But he expresses deep shame of those of us who affirm him as Christ, call ourselves after his name, and yet refuse to follow him in a vocation of being alongside. This, not suffering or the rejection it attracts, is shameful, abhorrent to God, contrary to Jesus, and contrary to our own souls as followers of his. And from the shame of God, who will deliver us?

NOTES

1. Michael Callen quoted in F. and M. Siegal, *AIDS: The Medical Mystery* (New York, Grove Press, 1983), pp. 182-3.
2. Bonaventure, *The Life of St Francis*, I.5, in Ewart Cousins, ed., *Bonaventure*, Classics of Western Spirituality, SPCK 1978; from Thomas of Celano, *Second Life*, 9.
3. Bonaventure, I.6; Thomas of Celano, I.17 and II.9.
4. cf. Leonardo Boff, *Saint Francis: A Model for Human Liberation* (SCM 1981), pp. 23-8.
5. For an investigation of the insulating effects of theodicy, see Ken Surin, *Theology and the Problem of Evil*, Oxford, Blackwell, 1986.
6. Seymour Kleinberg, 'Dreadful Night', in *Christopher Street* #76, 1983.
7. Dennis Altman, *AIDS and the New Puritanism* (Pluto Press, 1986), p. 59.
8. cf. Altman, p. 25.
9. For further discussion of the relationship between societal attitudes and shame, and its distinction from guilt, cf. John Rawls, *A Theory of Justice*, (Cambridge, Mass., Harvard University Press, 1971), pp. 442-6.
10. Nahum 3.6; Zechariah 9.7; Deuteronomy 7.26.
11. 'Natural Pride and Natural Shame', in Amélie Rorty, ed., *Explaining Emotions* (Berkeley, Los Angeles, and London, University of California Press, 1980), p. 368.

Lloyd

This story is told by a close friend of Lloyd's who had known him from childhood. Those closest to Lloyd have shared their reflections on his courage and growth with the storyteller. It is a story of a journey through adversity as Lloyd related to other people, and one which perhaps is appreciated more in retrospect, for only time allows a fuller understanding of pain. Not all are so lucky as Lloyd and his friends.

Lloyd was an assured, well-liked and relatively successful young person, who had built a good personal, social and professional life in London, before becoming ill and being diagnosed with HIV. He had always planned ahead; organizing his life, setting and accomplishing goals. His happy relationship with Simon, his partner who had shared his life and interests for some time, and with his family and friends, were enviable. Then came progressive illness, physical decline and hospital treatment, igniting a wide range of feelings and emotions, and forcibly changing the direction of Lloyd's life.

Much that happened was dramatically contrasting. Lloyd was a tenacious competitor. Once at school, several boys ganged up on his birthday, to give him a traditional 'bumping'. He didn't like this! With extraordinary physical will power, he resisted six people's efforts to hurl him through the air. He showed me the same spirit years later as he fought off two serious attacks of pneumonia to win for himself a near-two-year extension of life. During this remission, Lloyd spoke optimistically of future plans: to travel abroad, to see this or that, to move on and up at work. AIDS was a challenge to be resisted; Lloyd bravely kept up a pride in living: on a visit to his family he told his mother off for suggesting he wear the same clothes for two days running; little things of normal life were to be maintained. Death was pushed away, never discussed with his family and only rarely with others through a mutual fear of the great taboo.

Occasionally, glimpses of Lloyd's awareness of mortality would emerge. He told of the day in hospital the doctor told him AIDS had been confirmed. Lloyd put on a headphone set, and, hearing music by Sibelius, in his stunned shock he felt it waft over him with such impression that he instructed it to be played at his funeral, for which he wrote down other requests. Largely denying, but at moments conceding inevitability. Then towards the end, confined first to a chair, then bed, Lloyd appeared mainly calm and philosophical, as if his struggle was fought.

The attainments of it could already be seen. His illness had made Lloyd less able to cope with routine and equally shared aspects of life, yet more aware of people and relationships on another level. Being unable to drive and needing help with simple tasks, assistance in opening a door or going to the toilet, was demeaning and bitterly frustrating. Losing patience in furiousness at his limitations, Lloyd swore at Simon when unable to reach the telephone and answer a call, resentful at his loss of mobility. One evening throwing his dinner, brought by Simon, over the wall, another day in the park snapping irrationally at Jeff who had made him some sandwiches, 'I don't want them', then a little later meekly taking them. Biting the hand that feeds you—a classic symptom of frustration which Lloyd acknowledged—he was grateful to Jack, someone who encouraged Lloyd to shout and swear at him, for therapeutic value.

Yet, another side to the frustration of restriction and dependence was the time for reflection and awareness which this enforced opportunity gave. Lloyd saw more the joys of simple everyday things, human company and real values, so easily taken for granted otherwise. To see Lloyd showing fortitude and sensitivity alongside periods of wrath and despair, was to witness the growth of a whole, rounded humanity. Memories of Lloyd include his capacity during illness for savouring essentials, and enabling others to share them. A walk amid Hampton Court gardens is recalled by his parents, and similar occasions by others. The delight in spending time slowly, with someone who had to take his time; looking around, enjoying the scenery of a pretty location, just being in company.

Three weeks before his death, Lloyd was driven around northern beauty spots by Simon on a holiday tour he had been determined on. Tenacious again, making the most of the 'present moment', though completely unable now to move by himself, and sometimes in agony of discomfort and fits of depression. For the most part relishing the visual splendour of the countryside, but once making an outburst at the roadside when being washed took half an hour. Physically dependent on Simon and his vigilant family, Lloyd's loved ones were becoming more dependent on him. Lloyd's love for them was vivid. 'If it wasn't for you I would have nothing to live for', he said more than once. In the months before his passing, people felt their bond with Lloyd growing, and saw his sensitivity and insight into their own lives; from the richness of his unfolding experience he could lend his own sense of proportion to others' cares and concerns. It was a perspective of increasing self-knowledge, noticing a pattern and purpose to his life. 'I'm seeing things coming together, little things, all sorts of things making sense', Lloyd commented one day. The significance of events or circumstances grew clearer or more acceptable to him; 'I feel as if something or other is in control, guiding me.' Though not particularly religious, there was a marked spiritual development in Lloyd, a gaining of objectivity and maturity which was also a blessing for those near him. And so followed the tears of the dependants around the hospital bed in the last days and since, the pain of those bereft of Lloyd, who meant so much to them.

3

Members One of Another

Andrew Henderson

'I realize that this diagnosis of AIDS presents me with a choice: the choice either to be a hopeless victim and to die of AIDS, or to make my life right now what it always ought to have been.'

Graham has died of AIDS and the way he went about his dying has been an inspiration to his many friends, for somehow he was able to ride the tension between hope and optimism. Optimism that as a young man he might hold off premature death from a disease that realistically made him fear for his life; and hope that through reordering the way he spent his remaining time, whether it was to be long or short, he might discover the secret of how to live life to the full in the face of the present threat of death.

I knew Graham well. He was, like myself, a member of the network from which London Lighthouse emerged. We all knew that central West London held over half of the early UK incidence of AIDS, and London Lighthouse is accurately described as a unique and local service response. Now we have a magnificent building which houses not only a hospice unit but also a comprehensive array of interlocking services for people affected by HIV. It combines terminal and respite residential care with volunteer training for domiciliary support work and offers a range of counselling and group opportunities. The development of the project enjoys heartening support from a wide range of official and charitable bodies, as well as from the local community and the Churches.

I have been both the Borough's Director of Social Services and a local resident identified with the gay community. Reflecting on our experience from a Christian point of view and going behind the description of the services, I am struck by the way the creative power of Lighthouse has always radiated from the sense of new life that came to Graham; and this has been shared by many of us involved in the crisis of AIDS as an unexpected blessing. Lighthouse goes beyond compassion, because it is rooted in a shared experience of transformation.

In Chapter 1 of this book Stephen Pattison suggests connections between this type of 'born again' experience amongst people discovering they have HIV and the core Christian experience of what we sometimes call the resurrection life. To get to know people who have taken up this stance is exciting but also disturbing; for if those are to be our priorities too, then most of the common assumptions of a decent, well-ordered life will have to be questioned. At once it becomes tempting to defend our current order of priorities with the patronizing thought that this claim to new life is best understood as admirable bravado or whistling in the dark; or if we are analytically inclined we might suggest that denial has come into play. In fact, those of us who are involved with people living with HIV and with service provision have seen that this assertion of hopeful living can indeed sustain people through their dying; nor does the departure of the dead destroy the commitment of the living to go on reaching for true life in every available moment. What is more, this transformation of the AIDS experience from tragedy to opportunity may be shared by volunteers, service users and staff, whatever their HIV status. In this chapter I want to reflect on the corporate nature of this phenomenon and to interpret some implications for the Churches and beyond. For what is becoming clear is that AIDS is only an intense focus for issues that are universally with us.

It is noticeable that the ability to approach the diagnosis of HIV as an opportunity is usually mediated through membership of a support group or network of some kind. Before Lighthouse moved into its present 'cathedral', it had already grown into a living network or company of some hundreds of people affected by HIV. Many had been diagnosed HIV positive; some were friends, partners or family; others were service providers or volunteers who recognized early on that AIDS is an issue for everyone, whether or not we know we have the virus in our bodies. The development of Lighthouse is not unique in this respect: many of the AIDS organizations have developed from similar groups, and typically people with the virus have been among the founders and inspirers of the new organizations. What occurs in the best support networks is the creation of living groups; and of course knowledge and use of group dynamics is widespread in the Churches. What makes AIDS networks of particular interest and relevance to Christianity is the convergence of so many fundamental issues in AIDS, namely death and dying; loss and disability; sexuality, sexual orientation and the nature of loving relationships; rejection, marginalization and prejudice; poverty through loss of job, accommodation or income. Any group which finds a way to live with these issues must surely be closely related to the essentials of the Christian faith. A key characteristic of these groups is that they are not working just with their minds on understandings about AIDS, but together are plumbing the depths of fears and horrors, and emerging the other side with hope and with some sense that all can yet be well. Just how this is accomplished is difficult to discuss apart from the experience of such a group: an excellent exposition of the agendas of AIDS support networks can be found in a short book by Christopher Spence, the director of London Lighthouse.[1]

What AIDS then appears to confirm through the urgent drama of the apparently disastrous and wasteful deaths of many young people is that the saving experience for an individual is mediated through a saving community. Membership of a supportive group or network and frequent contact with the other members both informally and at meetings seem to be the means by which the crucial change of perspective comes about. These contacts must continue if the new stance is to be maintained and renewed through the ups and downs of the disease. Harvey Cox in discussing the connections between Buddhism and Christianity points out that Jesus did not preach a particular message: he himself was the message.[2] And it was presumably the experience of the early Christian communities that it was through meeting together in their common commitment to Jesus' way that they encountered and individually incorporated the reality of his living spirit—primarily via a group experience. So AIDS brings a timely reminder that Christians should be suspicious of any tendency to over-individualize or to privatize conversion, belief or spiritual practice. Our faith is characteristically about membership and sharing and looks to the coming of the Kingdom of God; and even though this metaphor may contain unfashionably hierarchical and sexist notions, it nevertheless does reach towards a social or community view of our ultimate destiny.

When I first began in social services, in good 1960s' style I held a rather naive belief in the welfare state as the demythologized inheritor of the Churches. I hoped that through the practice of organized love in our various services we would eventually bring in the Kingdom. Clearly the statutory services and the voluntary sector have taken forward the historic community welfare role of the Churches, but I no longer try to equate either the services or the Churches with Christianity. Now I see both institutions primarily as expressions of the old covenant of decency, law and justice rather than as vehicles of salvation, vessels of the spirit of freedom, or standard-bearers of victory over alienation and the fear of death.

So it is interesting to see how the AIDS networks which seem to be spirit-filled communities interact with the more formal AIDS organizations. Even while using the services, people with HIV frequently experience frustration at the way organizational considerations tend to occlude the original vision and aspirations. Nor is this primarily a consequence of the lack of resources. Compared to state responses to the AIDS crisis in the USA, for instance, the UK has done relatively well. The government has produced policies and funding to encourage local health and social services authorities to develop integrated services to meet the nature of the problem in their area. Built into these approaches is the intention that whenever possible those affected by AIDS should participate in the evolution and planning of services. Funding is available for self-help groups. Since the major incidence of AIDS in this country for the moment is amongst two socially marginalized groups, homosexual or gay men and intravenous drug users, it is understandable that there has been some reluctance from politicized liberationists to accept 'tainted' government money; but the offer is there at least for the time being. While health authorities have the main task of providing treatment, social services departments in London have a fairly sophisticated approach to domiciliary and community services for those affected by AIDS. It is generally recognized that voluntary provision may often be more acceptable than direct council service. Such political considerations should not be allowed to mask a more fundamental point for the Christian life; it is still the case, even where innovatory and sympathetic new organizations have emerged to meet the challenge of AIDS, including within them individuals with the virus at all levels, that support groups and networks continue to be experienced as vital. There may often be tensions and antipathy between small group members and the organizations they use. Something in the nature of organizations as they have to formalize themselves around issues of responsibility and accountability seems to take them predominantly into the area of the old covenant rather than the new. In London Lighthouse it has been a painful experience for the original founding group to recognize that innovations and new life may now come more often from informal groupings of service consumers rather than from those who so recently followed the pillar of fire in the vanguard of advance. Their task now is to ensure that their organization is properly established.

If there has been a lesson for the Churches to draw from all this it is that a Church taking the form of an institution or an organization should not expect itself often to provide more than the context within which living groups committed to the new covenant of love and freedom may emerge from time to time. Of necessity an organizational Church is primarily concerned with the old covenant, with ritual and with ordered living if it is to maintain itself. Communities of the spirit are most likely to be found at its margins and outside it altogether. This is not to denigrate the part played by the structured Church which increasingly shares the form of the public bureaucracies. To get our expectations clear is releasing and I believe that the old covenant of justice, stability and consistency is an essential prerequisite for the emergence of the life of the spirit. What this sort of understanding does not avoid is the disruption caused by the interplay between the old and the new. When new life does break in it will often bring thoroughly upsetting as well as inspiring consequences. This is costly in every sense for organizations which attempt to remain open to change, secular and ecclesiastical alike.

To move on now to address the question of the part the Churches can play in responding to AIDS at a community or congregational level, it is helpful to distinguish between different types of need. First, there is the most obvious call to offer pastoral care around and through the experience of death and dying. Second, well-organized home visiting linked with practical help in the home over such things as shopping, correspondence, cooking and cleaning can do a great deal to assist those significantly disabled by AIDS to remain at home. Often their carers and friends also need help to sustain themselves in what can be a very demanding time.

There is no need to rehearse again at length here the alienation from the Churches felt by many living with AIDS. What is absolutely clear is that the Christian faith implies a compassionate and loving response to both these types of need. That is not to say that the care offered should be without challenge; but it is simply not worth wasting time on the possibility that it might be Christian to make such help conditional in any way, let alone to withhold it. Most of us are only too well aware of the blocks within ourselves and in our church tradition that will inhibit us from giving generously of ourselves in this way. In spite of my close involvement I am constantly brought up short by the way I have internalized the fears and confusions around the issues raised by AIDS. So the message to everyone is clear: we must sort ourselves out and take the many opportunities offered in the programmes of organizations like London Lighthouse, CARA and the Terrence Higgins Trust to address our own agendas and to emerge with a little more clarity. Only then will we be free enough to be alongside our friends living with AIDS, not as some special entity called 'a Christian', but as the splendid human being Christ calls us to be: that is all that is required—and it is everything.

These two types of need, then, present no theological or practical problem. The parable of the Good Samaritan and our wide appreciation of the call to compassion establish it beyond any doubt that the Churches should be reaching out to everyone struggling to live with this terrible disease. But there is a third type of need which is all the more challenging for being less dramatic and closer to the issues of ordinary daily life. It is the need for close support and human friendship from people who share the commitment to make our lives and the world around us what we always hoped it could be. What I am raising now is the extent to which Christian groups and congregations are called to become involved with the social and support group activities of people affected by AIDS. For most people in this position acute health crises are only a small part of the picture and most people will be continuing with their home and work commitments as fully as they can in the face of the threat of the virus.

While working in the social services I often said to representatives of the local churches that while I appreciated that their projects aimed to meet the needs of vulnerable groups in the community, I felt they underestimated their potential as the largest community building agency in existence. The Churches have always found it relatively easy to offer care and compassion to the straightforwardly disadvantaged. These initiatives bring with them the danger of emphasizing the distinction between the helpers and the helped; there can be something distancing, if not downright patronizing in the helping hand stretched out by the strong to the weak. What the Churches find it much more difficult to do is to engage on an equal footing with others of good heart and serious intent around building up saving communities and exploring ways of sharing the life of the spirit. To apply this distinction to the AIDS phenomenon, it may be that the greatest challenge to Christian people comes at this third level of need which approximates to the need that draws most Christians into church membership in the first place. People with AIDS have gone ahead and have formed their own support networks. Some of us from Christian backgrounds realize we can discern the powerful working of the spirit in these groups and equate them with Christian cells or little churches. Many lives have been enriched, yet these networks are confined in large measure to AIDS issues and have within them the limitations that implies. People living with HIV can be short of friends outside the AIDS circle and often need contacts and ways of using their time that lift them out of the danger of pursuing an exclusive AIDS 'career'. Here is an opportunity for Christians to put into practice our aspiration to be truly 'members one of another', based on a real appreciation that 'we all have sinned and fallen short of the glory of God'.

Specifically, we have sinned and fallen short, in that few of us in Western societies are good at facing the precise issues that AIDS carries; issues of living with diminishment and early death, questions of the nature of sexual orientation and of close relationships, and of the wider meaning of our lives. Here in AIDS is a significant opportunity which might best be taken in practical terms by Christian groups asking one of the many experienced group facilitators with HIV to come and help them learn together from the AIDS experience. What would flow from that is not only the freeing of any blocks that individuals might have against taking part in care schemes; such courses would also help to make the Churches into the sorts of places where people with HIV, those at risk and the 'worried well', and those on the margins wanting support to live good lives would want to come. So AIDS can be a special opportunity for the followers of Jesus.

When the Church became a major social institution it was perhaps inevitable that it would primarily underwrite the best moral and ethical aspirations of society as a whole rather than play a consistently prophetic or innovatory role. Now that our post-modern and pluralistic age has little interest in the traditional place of the Church, it may be that we have a new chance to address the essentials of our faith. Jesus' way convinced his followers that he held the secret of how to live our lives to the full, divinely in fact, in the face of the realities of loss and suffering, and the ultimate certainty of death. Since denial of death is a major defence used by most people to allow us to find meaning in our lives from our day-to-day routines, it is not surprising that the Church as a social institution has so often played into this denial by offering a view of death as an easy transition to the next world, in fact scarcely an interruption of our individual existence. We should not give the Church or ourselves too hard a time for getting caught up into one of the traditional jobs of any major religion: to help people cope with life in an ordered and decent way. Jesus himself did not reject the religion of his day although he criticized some aspects of its practice; but then neither did he show much sign of wanting his way to be constructed into an alternative or higher religion.

It is ironical and perhaps it is a judgement on the Church for its secularization that it finds itself saddled with so much baggage that soon may be widely discarded by society at large. Don Cupitt has identified the addressing of sexism in the theology and structure of the Church as the key to unlocking our faith from the order of the past.[3] Out in the wide world, while awareness of the power of heterosexism has certainly spread, we are only at the beginning of understanding the revolutionary consequences of actually doing much to change the old order. Little wonder then that the Churches are no better than the rest of society at making sense of teaching about sexual and family relationships; not only have sex and sexual institutions been used to maintain patriarchy and to subjugate women, it is likely too that the inculcation of sexual shame and guilt are prime means whereby children and young people are kept under adult control. The whole area is very messy and no one piece of it can be satisfactorily addressed without opening ourselves to a total reorientation of our understandings. Jeanette Renouf explores this issue in more depth in Chapter 6.

In that AIDS brings together sex and death it offers an opportunity for Christian people to join with those facing a life-threatening disease to see what happens to accepted sexual conventions and prejudices when the near certainty of a long life is pulled away. It is a positive advantage in this situation that what is often involved is a mode of sexual being—homosexuality—that has been traditionally stigmatized by the Churches as sinful, and is marginalized by society in general. Since we know that rejected minorities tend to act out the fears projected upon them by the majority it is vitally important to hear what gay people living with AIDS say about the social role handed out to them. In the light of the priorities and urgency engendered by the closeness of death it may be that new moves will emerge towards modes of sexual being that question the hetero–homo divide and help to reintegrate this part of the body corporate. For this to happen homosexual people cannot do the work alone.

There is another aspect of AIDS pressing for attention. Although it is the case that the majority of people living with AIDS at present are homosexual men, there are growing numbers of people affected by HIV through blood or sexual contact as a consequence of the intravenous use of drugs by themselves or others. The transformation of death is key to the Christian stance; and while sexuality is ordinarily associated with procreation and enjoyment of life, drug misuse and dependency are already linked in the popular mind with the risks of self-destruction and early death. The life-styles of those caught up into drug addiction are often chaotic and at odds with the law. Once again the Churches should not be too self-critical if they find it hard to reach out to drug users. No one is very effective at this type of outreach except on a small scale: the statutory social and health agencies have long ago recognized that small and flexible voluntary organizations have a much better chance of coming alongside the drug culture than have the welfare bureaucracies. Within the AIDS agencies themselves how most effectively to involve drug users in their programmes is a continuing and largely unanswered question.

There is something about the nature of drug dependency that relates it to the dynamics of religious groups. Anyone privileged to have attended meetings of Alcoholics Anonymous will know that the power of the group to break the addiction and to heal and restore comes through intense experiences of personal confession and testimony. Members are expected to attend regularly and to open themselves trustfully to the group both for challenge and for support. What often follows can be like a conversion experience, and it looks as though psychological dependence on the group takes the place of biochemical dependence on the drug, in this case alcohol. For Christians to be asked to consider the possible links between church membership and drug addiction is somewhat analogous to a stockbroker being asked how his activity relates to gambling. It is not a welcome question. Yet, to put the point more positively, the phenomenon of drug dependency might be interpreted as a protest at the margins at the current secular heresies of individualism and the glorification of independence. When our physical make-up renders us dependent for our existence on a reliable supply of food, a constant supply of water and a continuous supply of air, it seems unlikely that we will experience our fullest spiritual potential by concentrating on independence. Somehow the concept of dependence needs rehabilitation and perhaps AIDS offers a contribution to this process. For Christians who continually wrestle with what it may mean to become a mature person, free yet created, it is a chance worth seizing. The membership of many church congregations involves such an undemanding level of commitment that the barrier through into new life is unlikely to be broken by this means. Perhaps that is why house churches and other more intimate Christian groupings have become so popular. People are hungry for the freedom that lies the other side of significant emotional commitment to a fuller life than can be achieved either individually or through friends and family and job.

Prescriptions for action from this line of thought are not so clear. For society as a whole the main threat of AIDS to the majority of our population of young, sexually active people is through the drug user route. Some Christians will have the chance to contribute to preventive strategies which will surely involve the formation of satisfying and attractive groups to join. For Christians, though, there is the prior step to take for ourselves in response to some of our number who are living with HIV. Their plea is that we find ways to shift whatever gets in the way of our being alongside one another. It is a matter of finding the courage to make a living reality of the knowledge we already have—that we are most fully ourselves, the people God made us to be, when we are members one of another; not dependent or independent but spiritually interdependent through a shared commitment, probably fostered within the life of a network or small group. AIDS is frightening and fear undermines closeness between people; the way to transform AIDS must be to make it the occasion for our salvation, so that we begin to live in real interdependence with each other, and are ready to explore the consequences of what that might mean.

Reflection, then, on the way in which the crisis of AIDS can link with Christian practice suggests that it must first be in the common endeavour to discover true life by living each day 'as if thy last'. This learning to live in the present moment is described by those who grew close to Lloyd, whose story precedes this chapter. The fact that AIDS is a death-threatening crisis offers that perspective to us all. We notice that the type of networks and groups that can turn around the experience of living with HIV bear a close resemblance to some Christian cells.

AIDS has made its first entry into our own society through two rejected minorities, homosexual men and intravenous drug users. If Christianity has a prime focus it is on our ways of relating, and the development of AIDS points us to sexuality and dependence as two prime areas for interpretation. And since they are presented through the experience of rejected groups, Christians are likely to find here a prophetic message. Sexuality and dependence embrace the interplay between our individuality and our common life; if we can take this opportunity to address them, we may dissolve at last what holds us back from becoming members one of another.

NOTES

1. C. Spence, *AIDS: Time to reclaim our power*, Lighthouse, Lifestory Publications, 1986.
2. H. Cox, *Many Mansions*, Collins 1989.
3. D. Cupitt, *Radicals and the Future of the Church*, SCM 1989.

John Shine

John Shine has been at the forefront of work with AIDS/HIV, as a nurse, since its appearance in London in 1981/2. He worked at St Stephen's Hospital, where many of the early cases were diagnosed, and became frustrated and alarmed by the denial of what he perceived to be a major health crisis. Conscious of the need for a hospice, a safe place, where people could come to be listened to, rest and die well, he joined forces with Christopher Spence and others to create the vision that became London Lighthouse. After working with Lighthouse for over two years, he moved on to set up a small neighbourhood-based counselling project, called 'The Red Admiral Project', in Earl's Court, London.

Having worked with many hundreds of people with AIDS/HIV, their lovers, partners and families, I have been asked about my experience of the Church and its repsonse to HIV/AIDS. In tackling this question, it might help if I explain my own approach and viewpoint about AIDS/HIV.

People with the disease are cast as victims and have what I see as two choices: either to buy into the victim role, or see this dis-ease as an opportunity to empower themselves and take charge of their life and death. I see my role as a facilitator of the process, walking alongside; not pulling from in front or pushing from behind. I can only do this work rationally, and function well, to the extent that I am supported: and by this I mean enabled to offload the feelings that get triggered in me during this close involvement. How can we give if we don't receive?

Which leads me to my observation of many Church members, who are expected to support by listening to others but do not get *well* listened to in return. There seems to be some assumption that, as religious representatives, they are bottomless pits, who somehow receive all their needs from some external power or divine influence.

They are further burdened by a tendency in others to invest them with some kind of mystical power. Knowing that all human beings are born inherently equal, how can it be that some possess these mystical powers and others don't? Any notion of a spiritual 'expert' maligns the truth that every human being has within them all they need to live their lives to the fullest. Quite simply, all that is required is that we listen well to each other. It's all very simple really.

Increasingly, I hear people with HIV/AIDS, particularly towards the end of their lives, expressing disappointment in their religious beliefs, often rejecting a religious funeral. I also observe that as people approach death and their physical bodies start to deteriorate, their spiritual and intuitive aspect grows, and they begin to review their lives and its wind-storms. Going back through childhood, they recall messages that some mystical force would transport them from life into death, taking them to a 'place called heaven'. During this review of memories, they come to episodes where they feel they hadn't lived in harmony with that which would contribute to their passport. I continue to notice immense disappointment and conflict.

The confusion is that, on the one hand they were aware of messages which judged some of their past behaviour as 'sinful', yet, on the other hand, knew at some deep level that they were completely good, had done nothing wrong, and that the childhood messages, though they *felt* real, weren't *reality*. At this stage of the dying process energy is no longer expended on trying to hold such tensions and contradictions in place. A new awareness of reality supersedes that which had been thought real, and maybe for the first time in their lives they feel betrayed by the lies they had been fed. Nature abhors imbalance and reality has to win out. Part of this reality is the realization that we die alone, even though often surrounded by many people.

How organized religion does well in its response to AIDS is that, despite its ambivalent attitude towards homosexuality, there are many individuals working within the Church, sometimes gay or lesbian themselves, taking very positive action; for example, organizations such as CARA and ACET, which have taken the initiative despite opposition.

My suggestion for how the Church can give the right support to people with AIDS/HIV is the same as for any institution dealing with this issue; that is, to provide plenty of opportunity for its own personnel to be listened to well; once again, how can we give if we don't receive?

My final thoughts on the matter concern what may well be an insurmountable difficulty. I think it is not possible for the Church to have a good response to AIDS. Organized religion finds it difficult to deal with homosexuality, so how can it have a healthy outlook on 'the gay plague', plus of course the newer aspect of intravenous drug users. Furthermore, I believe the only way forward in living with AIDS is for all affected to reclaim their full power as human beings. This is at odds with how organized religion works, which is to keep everyone powerless and in their place. Its personnel are controlled by doctrine and mystical beliefs and its followers are judgementally manipulated with threats and promises of 'heaven' and 'hell'. How can anyone in these circumstances reach a healthy self-acceptance and be able to accept others?

To change this would challenge the whole value-system of organized religion and would probably result in an organization bearing no resemblance to the Church that we know today.

4

New Showings: God Revealed in Friendship

Mark Pryce

It is the close of July, Gatwick airport. A stagnant mass of people is standing before the check-in desks of American airlines. The computers have shut down again. Long queues of travellers surrounded by heaps of bags. Meandering lines of people growing agitated, resentful as the waiting frustrates away their excitement and apprehension. All kinds of people. Families heading for Florida, their first trip to Disneyland. Students returning home for the summer guarding great taped-up boxes of books. Two elderly ladies attempting to manoeuvre a wheel-chair through the reluctant current of the waiting crowd. People bashing bags with trolleys as they try to make their way to somewhere impossible over the other side of the foyer. Tempers are getting bruised. All this technology, and no one's going anywhere fast.

Two lines away stands a tall, angular man. His hair is silver grey, cut short. His body is a streak of black, black from his neck to his shoes. Cassocked black. All his bags are black. His shoes too are black, of course. From the side he seems to be a kind of TV cleric—a Thornbirds Cardinal: fine profile, an aristocratic air. Indeed, as he turns very slightly to look about him, he shows the heavy gold of a chain flung across his chest, the bold cross of a bishop hanging over the breast buttons of his cassock. The large purple stone on his right hand. Every inch the prelate. As he stands he is very much alone, emerging from the sea of people around him. He has set himself apart, passing through his hands the black beads of a rosary. Silently his lips move round the prayers. Is he anxious about flying perhaps? He does not waste the waiting minutes; he practises his piety as he has been taught to do. It is almost as if he were queuing for another world, returning to some severe country very alien to our own.

Adjacent, almost beside him, are three men. Beyond the movements of their group stands the dark figure of the bishop. They are men in their forties, like him. Nothing very special about them, except that they are dressed as some gay men do. From their talking two are English and one American. The American does not look very well. Thin and grey in the face, his leather jacket hanging loose from his shoulders. Once he had filled his jeans, but not now. From his breathing one can tell that this journey is a physical strain for him. The three are saying goodbye. They are standing close together, arms about each other in an embrace and a hug. From time to time one will kiss the other and pat his back. One of them brushes away tears with the back of his hand, suddenly laughing at his own emotions, a little embarrassed perhaps. Embarrassed by the force of the feelings which have taken them in public, but not afraid of their emotions. Not afraid to demonstrate friendship and love and to stand close together as they say goodbye to a friend. Again they hug and make some joke about the journey, and their laughter draws the bishop from his prayers.

A discreet man, he does not want to stare too pointedly. His eyes slide towards the three then quickly look away. His fingers tighten round the beads as he jerks them a little quicker. He does not like what he has seen. Then his eyes are back again, suspicious, and he catches a trinitarian hug. He frowns disapproval, shaking his head. He turns away in a scowl of disgust, of terror, but in his own mind he cannot leave them alone. Again and again in the waiting line he looks then looks away and shivers his horror to himself. The lonely bishop is appalled and captivated as the three friends enjoy what is left to them.

Such imaginings may be completely misplaced, inaccurate interpretations of these people—if accuracy is ever appropriate or possible as an assessment in these things. Yet for me the bishop and the three friends are pictures of how we envision God. Two manifestations of divinity. The bishop's God is somewhere over the rainbow, way up high. He is distant, unapproachable, unengaged in human affairs except as the God of controlling power, looking down on us, watching us, watching our mistakes. He is the God of rules, the God who must be placated, the God who must be addressed in the correct forms and according to the correct rites. This God insists on the right language. This God is the rigid God, the God who loves laws and regulations, the God for whom we must conform. He is the God who deals only in individual souls; salvation is beyond the grave alone; suffering is to make us good, to get our place in heaven. With this God there is no satisfaction and no delight, but always disapproval. He is the moralizing preacher God, the ever-suspecting policeman God; the remote father God, the mother God whose expectations can never be met. The bishop's God is the model God whom we never manage to emulate. With this God we are always the failure.

This God is the judge God and most of us are afraid of him. We may be aware of how irrational he is, but beneath our confidences and our self-esteem, the fear of this God is lurking, undermining. He is the God who sends down punishments from on high. This God retaliates. He is the God who will zap me for writing these words, and you for reading them. He is the God who loves to keep a score of wrongs, particularly sexual misdemeanours. With this God you get what you deserve. If you are good then you enjoy good health. If you've got something bad then you did something bad to get it. With this God poverty is a penalty; disease and death are signs of his displeasure.

It is the activity of this God that many in the West see lurking about in AIDS. For many who pronounce themselves 'religious' and 'moral', the whole AIDS disaster is a display of this God's masterliness: the punishment of sin, the condemnation of sexuality, divine horror at the satisfaction of desire. AIDS has proved that homophobia is right, that it has God's seal of approval. More terrible is what goes on inside some of those who are wrestling with what it means to be living and dying with HIV. The guilt-God whisperings of those who are ill, the horrible assertions that sickness is deserved, that they brought it on themselves. The sense in which carrying a virus somehow validates all the negative experiences, rejections and condemnations that one has struggled to deny and overcome. Sometimes too, the loss of job, home, friends and family. The loss of health, independence, control. An affliction that seemingly could have come only from God.

Yet Jesus Christ contradicted this understanding of disease and disaster as God's punishments. He who was himself spurned, rejected and condemned showed that the condemnator-God is no God, for in Jesus very God goes the way of the cross. The gospel writers give a powerful impression of Jesus' teaching in this area. In Luke's Gospel Jesus contradicts the idea that God would choose to punish a specific group of people with painful death. Those who suffer disaster no more deserve to do so than those who escape. All have sinned and are in need of forgiveness:

> Those eighteen upon whom the tower in Siloam fell and killed them, do you think that they were worse offenders than all the others who lived in Jerusalem? I tell you, No; but unless you repent you will all likewise perish.
> Luke 13.4-5.

Or in John's Gospel, Jesus' meeting with the man born blind:

> As he passed by, he saw a man blind from his birth. And his disciples asked him, 'Rabbi, who sinned, this man or his parents, that he was born blind?' Jesus answered, 'It was not that this man sinned, or his parents, but that the works of God might be made manifest in him.'
> John 9.1-3.

Sickness is not a theatre in which to rehearse arguments about blame and divine retribution. God did not send this man blindness because of sin. Yet God is not outside the experience. God's light is to break out of this darkness, and in this adversity God's glory is to be revealed. The workings of God in the feared, despaired-of, cast-out sectors of human experience. For healing and not condemnation is what Jesus brings.

It is in this same terror of human disability and weakness, in fever and delirium, that Julian of Norwich received her *shewings* of God. She did not find the condemnation of God in her sickness, but the vision of God as love and peace. She discovered a new understanding of God as the one who delights in us, who longs to draw us ever closer. Not a God of anger, nor a God of displeasure, but a God whose mercy exceeds sin and whose grace exceeds our neediness:

> I could see no sort of anger in God, however long I looked. Indeed, if God were to be angry but for a moment, we could not live, endure, or be! Just as we owe our existence to God's everlasting might, wisdom and goodness, so by these same qualities are we kept in being. And although we wretches know from our own experience the meaning of discord and tension, we are still surrounded in every conceivable way by God's gentleness and humility, his kindness and graciousness. I saw quite clearly that our eternal friendship, our continuing life and existence is in God.[1]

For Mother Julian sickness has not revealed a vicious God, but God who befriends humanity. Sickness does not divide the guilty and the innocent; she finds a vision of the unity and harmony of all created being nurtured in the sustaining love of her Creator. Yes, pain and sorrow, conflict and brutality are very much part of the 'discords and tensions' of human being, but the picture she offers in her illness is of a God who is with us in our anguish, supporting us, defending us.

> I saw God to be our true peace, who keeps us safe when we are anything but peaceful, and who always works to bring us everlasting peace.[2]

Where is the peace of God, the assurance of God, the working of God in the pain and struggle of AIDS? The malicious scape-goatings in the press, the horrible degenerative illnesses, the untimely deaths; where is God to be found in these if not as angry outsider, plague-sender, law-enforcer God? What revelation of God, what new understandings of ourselves and of our fellow human beings break out of the AIDS situation?

This is where the image of the three friends speaks to me. For they speak to me of another way, of a God who is not far, a God who is not full of punishment. The three friends signal that love is in the heart of God, not hatred. In their support and care of one another they say to me: God is our friend and not our enemy. In their touch and in their mutuality they say that God is with us. God is by us. We can know God. Know God not only in an intellectual sense, but in the deep and intimate, sensate ways we come to know a lover or a friend. In our lovings and our friendship we can come to know God in what we experience. We can encounter God as the God who loves in those who cherish us, who loves in those we cherish. This is the God of the three; not a distant disapproving God, but a God who is close, who supports and strengthens and stands with us. God who challenges us to become whatever is most beautiful and excellent in us. God who nurses all that is most hurting in us. God, confronting all that is most hurtful in us. God who is near-by, strengthening, encouraging. When we stand together, when we love one another, it is then that we know this God.

The God whom the three friends picture for me is the true God, the Creator-God the one who delights in the body and takes pleasure in the physical. This is God encountered in Jesus Christ, the God who touches and who may be touched. Perhaps so much emphasis on an intellectual reception of incarnation has numbed us to the sheer, urgent physicality of people's encounters with Jesus in the Gospels. He is God surged up to, pressed against, grasped at, called out to. Jesus who takes fellow flesh into his arms, who lifts up little children, who is kissed at his betrayal, who makes his body metaphor. The power of God in feel, in breath and spit and mud and speech. The power of God which reaches out and sets the senses free. The God encountered in the body, the food, the fellowship of others. The worship of God in tears, caresses, in the ointment and the towel of hair.

The company of God is with those who are outside the bounds of accepted religious norms, those who have no place in the power structures of the day. The party of God is for those deemed indecent, contagious, inappropriate, unclean. It is with these people that God chooses to be located in Jesus of Nazareth. Present with them as their friend. For his relationships with them he was condemned as scandalous, 'the friend of tax-collectors and sinners' (Matthew 11.19; Luke 7.34). Yet his friendship is the complete revelation of God:

> No longer do I call you servants,
> for the servant does not know what his master is doing,
> but I have called you friends
> for all that I have heard from my Father I have made known to you.
> John 15.15.

This friendship is something much deeper than association, or even comradeship; the word for friend here is *philos*, beloved. To live in friendship is to keep Christ's commandment of love, and to abide in his love (John 15). In our friendships we come to know the friendship of God in Jesus, the befriender.

Very gently, very powerfully this friendship love can be wonderfully displayed in those living and dying with HIV and AIDS. Earlier in this book is the moving story of Lloyd told by one of his childhood friends. It tells of Lloyd's struggle with HIV as it forced changes in his life, Lloyd's anger at his growing dependence upon friends and family. Yet Lloyd's story is told as a friend's story, a kind of celebration of what the loved ones experienced together in and through AIDS. There is no denying the pain and the tragedy of Lloyd's dying. Though at the end Lloyd came to a sense of unity and purpose in life and death, Lloyd's death still seems cruelly premature to his friends. Few would want to describe this death as 'good' or glorify it. Yet in all the pain and mess and battle for dignity, in the love that they shared, it seems that Lloyd and his friends discovered a strange depth and quality of relationship, a richness of mutuality. Lloyd enjoyed loving care throughout his illness, painful and demeaning though this was for him at times. They also gained from him a new sense of perspective and an awareness of the sacredness and beauty of all life. Together as friends they have come to realize the miracle of life, life lived with others:

> The delight in spending time slowly, with someone who had to take his time; looking around, enjoying the scenery of a pretty location, just being in company.[3]

Surely this experience is gift, is blessing, the grace of the God who comes close. Grace found in friendship, found even in the misery of dying—perhaps there especially.

The commitment, support and mutual care of friends in 'the AIDS situation' has been the sustaining, transforming, salvific love of God in the spirit of Jesus Christ, divine befriender. Reflecting on the loss of his lover through AIDS one American gay man wrote these words:

> There were times when Todd's illness got the best of me. But that never lessened my love for him. He went away too soon. I have so much more inside to give him. All that is inside me right now Todd gave to me. He gave me extraordinary strength and courage. He gave to me love and understanding and compassion. Because of Todd everything I do, see, touch has new meaning. . . No one will ever know just how Todd has made this world a better place for me.[4]

In all the caring, all the shit and blood and sweat and anxious hours, in the anger and fear and rejection, in the laughter and the pleasure they have shared together, Chris senses his life to have been transformed and strengthened.

This healing, sustaining power is manifest in the friendships of support groups too, and in the more reciprocal 'professional friendship' between client/patient and care-giver. In this extract, for example, one man who is antibody positive tells of how a group of people in the same situation 'saved' his self-esteem.

> For the first time the people in that group . . . had a safe environment in which to talk, openly and honestly, about what had happened to them and how they felt about it. It was alright to cry at the things one had lost: relationships, security, freedom to choose how one lived one's life. It was alright to be angry about how society was treating you. It was alright to talk about fear.
>
> Some of us in that group went on to form the self-help group Body Positive, an example of a community of people infected with HIV helping and supporting each other, offering each other love and compassion, determined to challenge and contradict the notions that HIV was 'deserved', a moral contamination, and that people with HIV were 'finished'.[5]

Is such a community as this any less saving and liberating than a monastic foundation, or any religious community? Hasn't the women's movement shown us that it is in the friendship of groups that there comes restoration to the fulness of life, a rediscovery of the God-given dignity of each and every human being? The strength and courage to break out of abusive relationships; the discovery of self-esteem in being with one another, naming their oppression and their needs: flushing tranquilizers down the lavatories, lobbying the authorities for crèche facilities or a safe place to meet. The power for change in such groups rarely stays with individuals, but begins to transform communities or to form community out of chaos and void.

One of the most powerful stories in the Scriptures is of the friendship between two women, Ruth and Naomi. Mother and daughter through marriage, both now widowed, they befriend one another in the bleakest of situations: lone women in a patriarchal society, childless, hungry and poor in a time of famine. Their solidarity is complete:

> Entreat me not to leave you or to return from following you; for where you go I will go, and where you lodge I will lodge; your people shall be my people, and your God my God; where you die I will die, and there I will be buried. May the Lord do so to me and more also if even death parts me from you.
>
> Ruth 1.16-17

Through this friendship they transform disaster into celebration. It is through their friendship that God blesses them; there are no miracles of divine intervention in this narrative, but through their support of one another they play out divine grace and salvation. Naomi sends

Ruth to the fields where she meets her future husband. Ruth returns from her work with an apron full of grain for her hungry friend, who advises her how to clinch the marriage with Boaz and thus secure their happiness. Ruth has a husband, Naomi a grandson, and the harvest is gathered in. Community replaces isolation; fulness is restored; yet it is in Ruth that Naomi finds true joy, for 'your daughter-in-law who loves you . . . is more to you than seven sons' (Ruth 4.15). Women in solidarity overcome injustice and reverse catastrophe.

Their story is a model for us to experience and to celebrate God's kindnesses encountered through inter-personal relationships. Their covenant love is a pattern for our friendships and our ministries, an agenda for our prayer. To be going along with the other, accompanying them in life's journey, living with them what has to be lived, health and sickness, pleasure and pain, recognizing that all is provisional, ever moving on. Sharing our faith and our doubt and having eyes always to see where God is with us in the sojourning. Facing the ever-present reality of death, of the loss of the other, of the letting-go which does not signify rejection.

Let us look for friends in the horrific reality of AIDS, which is our reality, not for whom to blame. Let us be drawn into support and affirmation, not moral quarantining. Surely the task for the Church is to cease labouring so much over the construction of elaborate theodicies and clever 'moral responses' for AIDS, to cease all of that and simply to cherish who we are as persons: lonely, hurting, frightened, loving, healing, encouraging human beings who need each other desperately. Will we not then begin to see much more the revelation of the love of God in the love that men and women are finding together in supportive friendships: in the miracle of Buddying, London Lighthouse, the care of lovers, counsellors, and yes, even in the ministry of the Church? Will we not begin to see that sin is truly alienation, the rejection and loneliness of others? Will we not then begin to see that wickedness is in the prejudice which stigmatizes fellow human beings, promoting misunderstanding, forcing us apart and not together? Will we then not begin to abhor and end the exile which some have had to endure, pent-up within themselves and guilty, facing an illness alone and unsupported, their fears not listened to and their anger unheard? Will we not begin to affirm the supportive friendships of gay people and drug users alongside the accepted ties of family and marriage?

Sallie McFague suggests that in understanding God metaphorically as 'friend' we will come to share with God in the common purpose of saving the creation from destruction.[6] If we are the friends of Jesus the divine and human befriender, then AIDS compels our prayer and practical involvement. We must take our place alongside those living and dying with HIV, with those they have befriended, with those who have befriended them as they travel together through a largely unknown land. This is true ecumenism: the friends of Jesus in the Church joining all people of goodwill in the struggle to live and die in dignity. Not just in the Western nations, but throughout the world. This is the friendship which God longs to bring about.

In his novel, *The Plague*, Albert Camus explores this vision that the fight against disease, any disease, brings reconciliation. Here Rieux the atheist doctor and Paneloux the priest discover their solidarity:

> 'What I hate is death and disease—as you well know. And whether you wish it or not, we're allies facing them and fighting them together.' Rieux was still holding Paneloux's hand. 'So you see'—but he refrained from meeting the priest's eyes—'God himself can't part us now.'[7]

NOTES

1. *Revelations of Divine Love*, 49 (Penguin 1966), p. 138.
2. ibid.
3. Lloyd's story is on page 32 of this book.
4. Shelp, Sunderland and Mansell, ed., *AIDS: Personal stories in pastoral perspective* (Pilgrim Press 1986), p. 129.
5. Jonathan Grimshaw, 'Being HIV Antibody Positive', *British Medical Journal* 1988.
6. See her *Models of God*, (SCM 1987), ch. 6.
7. A. Camus, *The Plague* (Penguin 1979), p. 179.

Adrian

For about a year after my diagnosis I was in a sort of depressive stage of denial about it. I tried to carry on with my current life-style, working and preoccupied with my painting. But, gradually, I was filled with a lot of anxiety. I remember being terrified every time I got a cough—it was hard to cope with what was happening to me. I was helped tremendously by co-counselling. I think that the key thing for me has been the experience of being accepted and supported. I am very aware that I have obtained some sort of balance through letting out my emotions. It doesn't mean that I am happy all the time—I do get scared and angry and upset. I suppose that is all part of it.

Out of fear, people need something to believe in, something that will help us to make sense of the chaos. Perhaps all religions, political credos, holistic therapies, philosophies and psychologies, are attempts to deny death. 'Men fear death like children fear the dark', one of the classical poets wrote, and it sent a shiver up my spine when I first read it aged thirteen. Death is the great unknown but, by looking at man's behaviour through history, it is simultaneously the great explanation. If we reject natural death we are also rejecting natural life.

An HIV diagnosis presses all those buttons, and asks all those big questions: Why are we here? What will happen when I die? Is there a God? The big questions. But most of all it presses the button of fear. Will death be endless night? Endless pain? Or perhaps worse than that: Endless nothing?

I remember the first time I was really made aware of the possibility of my own death. At age twelve I went to a Planet of the Apes movie; the film ended with the destruction of the earth by the detonation of a nuclear bomb; aptly named the 'Doomsday Bomb'. That night I couldn't sleep—I really had the fear. The lies he tells, the confusions he creates, the contortions each man performs in order to avoid that fear and deny death's threat are the seeds of this world we have created. Empires: political, economic, artistic, whatever, are all built so as to survive us and render us immortal and contradict the apparent meaninglessness of existence. Crazy, irrational religions and philosophies using some promise of immortality and salvation to impose intolerance, persecution and, of course, to maintain the power of the élite.

I believe that the only way any of us can go forward, the only way we can create anything of value is by looking right into that void, right into that fear, feeling it, going through it—raging, screaming, crying—it won't kill you! As one man said, 'We have nothing to fear but fear itself.' Few listen and fewer still understand. Only once we've been through the fire can we see clearly, act rationally and, most important of all, truly love one another right up to death.

I still have my idealism and my hopes about the way I would like the world to be. Perhaps people will never live together in a community, co-operatively and in harmony. Yet somehow I believe that everyone from the most cynical stockbroker right down to a little child knows on some level that this is the way things are supposed to be. Perhaps a real and true response to AIDS can help to create a better world, a truly supportive, loving community where people can be creative together.

5

'The Carnality of Grace': Sexuality, Spirituality and Pastoral Ministry

Kenneth Leech

> It is somewhat difficult in today's world to relate one's Christian spirituality to decisions involved in living as a sexual being.[1]

So we read in the report *Sexuality: a divine gift* which caused a certain amount of fuss in the Episcopal Church of the USA two years ago. When I read those words, it brought to mind the words of Sir Arthur Streeb-Greebling on Peter Cook and Dudley Moore's album 'Not Only But Also'. Sir Arthur, who had spent his life teaching ravens to fly under water, when asked whether it had been a difficult task, replied, 'I think "difficult" is an awfully good word.' 'Difficult' is an awfully good word. But it does spring to mind as being the experience of many of us in the conflict and struggle betwen sexual and spiritual needs, desires and longings.

And yet it is, to say the least, rather odd that this should be so in a religion of incarnation, a religion which places a high value on matter, on the flesh, on the physical. The incarnational and sacramental religion and Church does seem to experience real and continuing difficulty in dealing with issues of human sexuality.

So we need to begin any consideration of the sexual and spiritual lives of pastors by recognizing the ambivalent record of the Christian tradition in the area of sexuality. The persistence of the gnostic Manichean tradition of the inherent sinfulness of the flesh has left its devastating and subtle effects on those 'mainstream' traditions which have officially repudiated it. Christian orthodoxy has never really rid itself of the gnostic influence. From Clement of Alexandria and Origen through Augustine and down to our own day, the dualism of spirit and matter has characterized much, maybe most, Christianity. Rachel Hosmer has written of Augustine:

> His view of sexuality is negative, guilty and shame-ridden. For Augustine the essence of the fall of the first human couple was the loss of rational control over the body, particularly over the phallus. To think that lust can

be tamed is a delusion. So for Augustine the sex act, which is not under the control of the rational mind and will, but seems to take place on its own, is sinful and transmits original sin to every child that is born of the flesh.[2]

It is largely because Augustine saw sin as natural to humankind, and associated its transmission specifically with *concupiscentia* and with sexual intercourse, that the Eastern Churches refuse to recognize him as a doctor of the Church or as one who teaches within the authentic tradition.

It is dangerous then to dismiss the gnostics as an aberration of the Christian past. There is an entry in one dictionary under the heading 'Encratites' which reads: 'An early Christian sect which held that original sin was transmitted through sexual intercourse. Extinct.' But the gnostic tradition is not extinct. It has entered deeply into Christian tradition and continues to damage Christian witness.

A related aspect of the ambivalent Christian record is its dread of women. There is a deep-rooted gynophobia within the Church which distorts theology, spirituality and ethics. Throughout the tradition women represent passion, the irrational instinctive realm of carnality. As daughters of Eve, they constitute a perpetual source of temptation. Medieval canonists debated whether married couples should receive Holy Communion if they had made love the previous night. St Bernardine of Siena held that it was a mortal sin not to abstain from sexual intercourse before Communion. Most of the references to women in early canon law are to do with their exclusion from the sanctuary and from contact with priests. For, as representatives of the lower, carnal nature, they were sources of contamination to those identified as holy.

It is not surprising that, as a consequence of so deep a disgust at human sexuality, there is often a profound unease in coping with sexuality pastorally. That is itself a manifestation of the conflict with which I began: for sex and the spirit are not seen to belong together. Sex only figures in the pastoral arena in the form of sin. Yet the pastoral relationship is, by its very nature, one which involves sexuality, and the ability of the pastor to be at ease with both his/her own sexuality and that of the other person in the relationship, is of central importance. Nor is it conceivable that 'spiritual direction' or 'the cure of souls' could occur in sexual beings without any attention to that central dimension. 'The soul' does not float freely.

And, of course, there is the continuing, and perhaps increasing, evidence of a type of religious zeal and fanaticism in which 'the fear of flesh and politics'[3] assumes sinister and reactionary forms. The deep disgust at sexual desire and tenderness, a disgust often linked with promiscuity and sexual exploitation of a violent kind, is central to most forms of fascism. The recent resurgence of homophobia is clearly connected both with crude right-wing 'fundamentalism' and with developments akin to a kind of creeping fascism within the Christian world. In both the USA and Britain, it is correct to warn that 'in the age of AIDS, gay and lesbian people remain the most vulnerable targets of Christian Right venom, which is likely to spread along with the epidemic'.[4]

So it is important to approach this area with penitence and caution, as well as a recognition of the dangers. The way that Churches have handled sexuality has been a cause of great suffering and scandal to many people. For the religion of incarnation has been presented as cold and lifeless, lacking in passion, in human warmth and tenderness. In Edwin Muir's famous line, 'The Word made flesh is here made word again.'[5] When Nietzsche commented that he could only believe in a God who could dance, he spoke for many who could not find such a God in Christianity.

And the truth is that many Christians have found their own tradition deeply deficient in its ability to cope with sexuality otherwise than as problematic. One of the best statements of the central problem was made by Sam Keen in 1970. Under the heading 'The importance of being carnal', Keen wrote:

> What has happened to me? How am I to understand this warmth and grace which pervades my body? As I begin to reflect, I realise that neither the Christian nor the secular culture, in which I have been jointly nurtured, have given me adequate categories to interpret such an experience. Neither has taught me to discern the sacred in the voice of the body and the language of the senses. In the same measure that Christian theology has failed to help me appreciate the *carnality of grace*, secular ideology has failed to provide me categories for understanding the *grace of carnality*. Before I can understand what I have experienced, I must see where Christian theology and secular ideology have failed me.

Keen goes on to speak of a 'deep seated suspicion of the carnal' within the Christian Church. And yet an incarnational spirituality must testify to the truth that grace is carnal, that healing comes through the flesh.[6]

If we are to undertake this necessary process of renewal, we need to recognize the major obstacles in our path, two in particular. One is to do with who make up the participants in the process, one to do with the level of engagement. Let me explain.

Much discussion in the institutional Church about sex—or about anything for that matter!—seems to take place in exclusively or overwhelmingly male, often clerical male, groupings—in some parts of the Church, exclusively celibate clerical male groupings. The systematic exclusion of women's experiences, reflections, struggles and perspectives, combined with the discussion, often compassionate, of gay men as if they were not present, and the overpowering non-recognition of Christian lesbians, renders most of this discussion partial and unbalanced. It is essential that the experience of those individuals and groups who have been systematically excluded are brought into the context of pastoral reflection.

Secondly, much Christian discussion of sexuality, as of politics, starts from an idealistic approach about what should be, rather than a realist or historical materialist anlaysis of what is. So the rhetoric of sexuality often fails to connect with the reality of people's lives and loves. Compare the utterly unreal way in which 'the family' is discussed in much Christian writing. Yet in many parish communities the model nuclear family, one man, one woman, who have never been married to anyone other than each other, and two children, does not exist. No personal strategy which is based on illusion can be of real service to people.

Or take that report *Marriage and the Church's Task* (1978) in which it is said of marriage that it 'cannot be too highly valued', although Jesus clearly said that the demands of the Kingdom of God would bring about conflict and division within families. Marriage is called a 'foretaste of God's kingdom', presumably that same Kingdom in which they neither marry nor are given in marriage. The man who used his recent marriage as an excuse did not taste of the heavenly banquet. The marital commitment is said to be 'total and unreserved', one in which we 'give everything and receive everything'—language which in the New Testament is reserved for the Kingdom of God. Such language is well meant. It is intended to present a 'high' view of marriage and of sexuality. But such a view is not only too high to be attained, it is utterly contradicted both by human experience and by theological tradition. Human experience shows that sexual relationships are enormously varied and do not conform to, or deviate from, a simple norm. Theological tradition points to the fact that the marital relationship is one among a number of types of commitment, none of which, apart from that to God and his Kingdom, can be seen as 'total and unreserved'.

Yet the persistence of idealist views of sexuality makes a Christian engagement with the realities of flesh and human passion more difficult, and creates a spirituality which is at several removes from the human condition.

Christian spirituality at its best is materialistic, incarnational, a spirituality of the whole person in communion. It is never a static essence, always a movement. It can, however, only be a liberating movement if it is formed and directed by a genuine materialism, rooted in the truth of incarnation, oriented towards human and creational wholeness. It is materialistic, believing that creation is the primal sacrament, that God is known not through 'unspoilt' matter but through matter which is itself in need of redemption. That is the meaning of the eucharistic offertory. It is incarnational, for, as Irenaeus said, if the flesh is not saved, the Lord has not redeemed us.[7] It is a spirituality of the whole person in community. Here the words of Gregory Nazianzen need to be grasped and interpreted for our day: 'What he [Christ] has not assumed, he has not healed'.[8] It is essential that the whole of human nature is saved. But human nature is sexual and social nature. Later generations of Christians failed to ask what Gregory's maxim meant for the understanding of sexuality. We are still struggling with the issues of social grace and social transformation.

In fact the tendency to see sex and the passions as a part of the 'lower nature' and to associate the image of God with mind and reason (the 'higher nature') was powerful and persistent. It has been reinforced from one generation to another. In our own day the New English Bible, by translating 'flesh' as 'lower nature', has perpetuated the long entrenched misunderstanding. The whole concept of a 'lower nature' is a Greek, not a biblical, one. In New Testament thought, 'the flesh' means unredeemed human nature. There is no hint here of the dualism which was later to enter and distort the understanding of the human person. Yet dualism and the denial of human sexuality were not actually victorious. In the thirteenth century, both Aquinas in the West and Gregory Palamas in the East stress the central place of the passions. Palamas insists that soul and body together constitute the image of God. The body and the emotions share in the divine nature: 'The passionate forces of the soul are not put to death but transfigured and sanctified.'[9] Aquinas also says that the passions are the subjects of virtues.[10] Most emphatic of all the medieval theologians is Julian of Norwich in her insistence that our substance and our sensuality are in God. Together they form our soul.[11]

It is essential to stress this, for we will never take sex with joyous seriousness if we continue to see our sexual lives as irrelevant to our spirituality, or if *eros* and *agape* are seen as wholly different. In early Orthodox theology love for God is seen as essentially erotic love, insatiable desire. Patristic writers such as John Chrysostom and John Climacus insist that physical human love is analogous to divine love. Chrysostom sees God as 'more erotic than bride and groom' while Climacus speaks of the love of God as an 'abundance of eros'. Symeon the New Theologian describes the relationship with God as intercourse and speaks of sleeping with Christ.[12] It is important to recover this tradition and to reject the modern idea that divine love is utterly disconnected from human sexuality, or that 'the lusts of the flesh' are inherently sinful. Rather should we hold, with the late Frederick Hastings Smyth, that 'a proper human eros catches into itself rationally a proper animal lust' while eros itself is subsumed into agape.[13]

The problem is that it is possible to accept these truths at a head level. The worst place to sort out sex is in the head. An incarnational theology is not simply a cerebral grasp of christological dogma. It is an acceptance of the solidarity of my flesh with the flesh of Christ and of all people, a recognition of the material and carnal character of grace and of the spirit. And this must involve a break with that element in Christian spirituality, associated with such writers as Thomas à Kempis, that sees human nature as getting in the way of union with God.

Christianity, however, is a faith not only of incarnation but of transfiguration and resurrection. The transfiguration of Christ anticipates both his resurrection glory and the transfiguration of humanity and of the creation, which will be set free to enjoy the glorious liberty of God's children (Romans 8.21). But it is humanity in all its complex nature which is transfigured and raised up. Resurrection is a 'further clothing', the swallowing up of mortality in a more abundant life (2 Corinthians 5.4). The spirit works with, and upon, an already existing physical nature. Paul is emphatic that 'it is not the spiritual which is first but the physical, and then the spiritual' (1 Corinthians 15.46). The Christian hope is not of the immortality of disembodied souls, nor is it the creation of a wholly new personality. There is continuity as well as contrast and change. But what is the effect of the resurrection process on sexuality? The main tendency has been to see this effect in terms of transcendence, yet that can only mean a move to something greater, not a leaving behind of something inferior. In fact transfiguration and resurrection are implicit and latent in the incarnation, the taking of humanity into God.

It is this approach to humanity and the world which makes all the difference between a religion of life and resurrection and a religion of death and preservation. We can see how this is closely linked with our approach to sexuality if we look at three symbols of Christian mysticism: fire, the dark night, and union with God. All are symbols of transfiguration.

Fire is a common theme in the mystical writers. The human person is said to be aflame with love. This is the language of wildness, of ecstacy, of terror. Our whole being is said to be on fire. Thus St John

Climacus addresses God with the words, 'Now thou hast ravished my soul. I cannot contain thy flame.'[14] We find the same language if we read St Symeon in the tenth century or Richard Rolle in the fourteenth. It is the language of 'fiery lovers', language which is clearly physical and passionate. To be aflame for God is to be a whole person. The imagery of orgasm and intoxication is used not as a contrast but as a pointer to something even more exhilarating and wonderful.

But a religion which is suspicious of the emotions and the erotic will be concerned to suppress these manifestations. One late nineteenth century clergyman in Cornwall blamed the rise in illegitimate births in the village on the influence of Methodism which encouraged ignorant peasant girls to give way to their emotions. Sensuality, passion and wildness are threats to the decent order of religion. They are seen as belonging to the 'lower nature', the flesh. But this is seriously to misunderstand the language of 'flesh' in the New Testament which is about sin and fallenness, not about intensity of feeling and passion. The 'living fire of love' makes men and women more, not less, passionate. But a religion which fears the erotic will also fear the mystical. The recovery of the mystical dimension is a necessary element in the recovery of warmth, humanity and compassion in religious life. Without a sense of the 'living flame of love', religion becomes dry, cold and repressive.

Let us take next the symbol of the dark night as described by St John of the Cross. Its central characteristic is to be out of control. But it is in sexual union that human beings are most aware of the creative as well as the terrifying potential in loss of control: a sense of mysteriousness combined with pain, and the darkness of exploration. Common to both a profound sexual relationship and the contemplative experience of the dark night is the sense of vulnerability. Karen Lebacqz[15] calls us to develop a theology of vulnerability. But much religion, fearful of vulnerability, of weakness and of loss of control, terrified by the release of psychic and spiritual energy, whether through sexual or mystical passion, is concerned to maintain control, to compartmentalize, to ensure security and safety. So in preserving its security it also preserves its immaturity.

Rollo May sees the central problem in sexuality today not in repression but rather in loss of feeling, lack of passion. Sex, he argues, has become a tool, an aid to performance, but in the process it has become banal and has been robbed of its power. 'We are in a flight from eros—and we use sex as the vehicle for the flight.'[16]

The mystical language of union with God is full of phallic imagery of penetration, full of sighs and moans and the poetry of lovers. It is extravagant, extreme, dangerous language, bordering on the heretical.

It is the language of lovers. So those Christians who are threatened by the explosive and subversive power of the mystical retreat again and again to the safe conventions and comfortable forms in which they can protect themselves from the living God. In this way religion which fears sexuality through which human love is manifested becomes unable to relate to God the source of all love.

I suggest that the mystical and the prophetic dimensions of Christian spirituality and discipleship both depend on a right valuation and integration of our sexuality. For both mysticism and prophecy depend on passion, on self-giving, on the integral union of heart and head, on a profound liberation of the personality. A failure to take our sexual nature seriously results in the mysticism of deranged religiosity and the politics of fanaticism.

Our potential for liberation, for the transfiguration of personality, depends on our openness to God and to the possibility for change. And here our theology of grace is of critical importance. Much Western spirituality has worked with a two-planes theology of nature and supernature. Grace is seen as extrinsic to nature. But the notion of supernatural was unknown to the Bible and the ancient Church. Eastern theology, as expressed today by Evdokimov and Meyendorff, stresses the presence of grace in the creative process, and sees human beings as deiform by nature. This openness to God, the potential for union with God, is not a supernatural gift but is the core of our nature.[17] To follow one's own true nature is to move towards God. But as sexual beings, by our nature, we can only move towards God in a way which fulfils and manifests our sexuality. For that which is not assumed is not healed.

A spirituality which takes human sexuality with theological and pastoral seriousness (as well as with theological and pastoral fun!) will not see sexual desire as a problem to be dealt with, but as a gift, as the raw material of holiness and creativity. It will be a spirituality of liberation which recognizes the close link between the policing of desire and the repressive machinery of society as a whole. So a spirituality which takes sexuality seriously will take politics seriously also. It will be a spirituality which is not afraid of passion, of darkness, of mystical union, not afraid of adventure and risk. It will be a spirituality which recognizes that human sexuality is an area where we do not know all the answers.

We will make progress only if women and men, people of different sexual orientations and in different relationships, see each other as comrades and not as threats to each other's identity, and seek to explore common ground together. And this means ceasing to fear one another. The New Testament teaches that fear is cast out by perfect love (1 John 4.18). So we all need to become lovers. Alan Jones, in an article called 'Are we lovers any more?', speaks of the loss of passion after ordination.[18] We must not be afraid to use that term. For it is by becoming lovers that we can begin to understand and express our sexual natures. It is by becoming lovers, and only by becoming lovers, that we can come to know God who is the source of all love.

To the gnostic both the flesh and the *polis* are threats to pure religion. Both are sources of contamination, zones of imperfection. We need to see the link between our sexuality and our politics. The policing of desire is a necessary part of the apparatus of a repressive state. Those who see changes in responses to sexuality as subversive are quite correct. Personal and political liberation are indivisible. And so I want to end with the suggestion that in our response to AIDS we are actually responding not only to a crisis which affects people and communities external to us, but to a crisis in our own understanding of life and loving, a crisis from which many of us will not emerge whole. But perhaps as a result of our wounds and our brokenness, and the bafflement we experience, in the end we will be better pastors.

NOTES

1. *Sexuality: a divine gift* (Task Force on Human Sexuality and Family Life, Education for Mission and Ministry Unit, Episcopal Church of the USA, 1987), p. 1.
2. Rachel Hosmer, *Gender and God: love and desire in Christian spirituality* (Cambridge, Mass., Cowley Press, 1986), pp. 73-4.
3. R. A. Lambourne, 'Personal reformation and political formation in pastoral care', *Journal of Pastoral Care* 25: 3 (September 1971), reprinted in *Contact* 44 (Spring 1974), pp. 30-8.
4. Sara Diamond, *Spiritual Warfare: the Politics of the Christian Right* (Pluto Press 1989), p. vi.
5. Edwin Muir, *Collected Poems* (Faber 1960), pp. 228-9.
6. Sam Keen, *To A Dancing God* (Fontana 1970), pp. 142ff. See the whole chapter, 'The importance of being carnal: notes for a visceral theology', pp.141-60.
7. Irenaeus, *Adv. Haer.*, 5.2.
8. Gregory Nazianzen, *Ep.* 101.
9. Gregory Palamas, *Hagioritic Tome* (PG 150: 1233B). See also *The Passions, the Virtues and the Fruits of Spiritual Devotion* (PG 150: 1043-88) and *Homily 33* (PG 151: 412-24); John Meyendorff, *St Gregory Palamas and Orthodox Theology*, Crestwood, NY, St Vladimir's Seminary Press, 1974.
10. For a critique of Aquinas see Roger Haight, *The Experience and Language of Grace* (Dublin, Gill & Macmillan, 1979), pp. 57-75.
11. Julian of Norwich, *Revelations of Divine Love*, 55-6.
12. See John Chryssavgis, 'The notion of divine eros in The Ladder of St John Climacus', *St Vladimir's Theological Quarterly* 29.3 (1985), pp. 191-200.
13. Frederick Hastings Smyth, cited in T. M. Brown, *Metacosmesis: the Christian Marxism of Frederick Hastings Smyth and the Society of the Catholic Commonwealth* (University of Toronto D.Th. thesis, March 1987), p. 40.
14. John Climacus, *Ladder* 30.18.

15. Karen Lebacqz, 'Appropriate vulnerability: a sexual ethic for singles', *Christian Century*, 6 May 1987, pp. 435-8.
16. Rollo May, *Love and Will* (W. W. Norton 1969), p. 65.
17. Paul Evdokimov, *L'Orthodoxie* (Neuchatel, Delachaux et Nestle, 1959), pp. 88–90; John Meyendorff, *Christ in Eastern Christian Thought* (Crestwood, NY, St Vladimir's Seminary Press 1975), p. 11.
18. A. W. Jones, 'Are we lovers any more?', *Theological Education* 24.1 (Autumn 1987), pp. 9-29.

David Randall

David Randall has been the pastor at CARA since 1988. He is an Anglican priest who worked for seventeen years in the East End and Notting Hill, London. He was diagnosed HIV positive in 1988.

There are three things that I want to bring to the Church. Two of them have always been there: my priesthood and my sexuality; and now I want to bring the virus to the Church. When I got the virus I said that I must use it as a 'gift'. There is a sense in which who we are is the gift that we bring and those three things are very important parts of who I am, so it is something I want to bring and use to help other people face the challenge of HIV for themselves. I don't think I have the answers but I do think I have the means of helping people respond to the challenge.

AIDS may actually be an opportunity to point the Church to love; the real nature of loving which is not about morals or about rules. If we look at what the secular message of good news is, from places like the Lighthouse Community, we discover a prophetic message of unconditional love. I believe Christ himself was the model of unconditional love, and that part of HIV's challenge to us is to demand that we look at our lives and try to discover what they are meant to be. There is a tension and paradox between the doctrine of creation and our understanding of original sin and the fall. I wonder if we haven't affirmed the intrinsic value of creation and people enough and that our concentration on sin and the fall leaves people with a tremendous sense of guilt and shame. The Church has not always been very good at helping people to see their intrinsic value; it is true that it is in dying that we are born but that has got to be seen against the context of a good and loving Creator who affirms that sexuality, sensuality and humanness are part of the wonder and beauty of Creation.

I think that it is difficult for us to come to terms with ourselves as sexual human beings. Sexuality must be on everybody's agenda. We find all kinds of excuses for not dealing with sexuality as part of the way we are and the way we act. It is very human, a very basic part of living and dying that preoccupies us a lot of the time. I have stood up in church groups as a priest, as a gay man and as being HIV positive and talked about living with the virus and discovered that people have got very angry with me. I think that they would have been much happier if I had been in a hospital bed, if I had gone away to die. Then they could pity me and pray for me and do good to me. This is an evasion, a running away from their own fears about disease, sexuality and death.

I think the Church could help by creating places of openness and love in every community where people are able to share what is at the heart of their lives, so that sex, hopes and fears about death don't have to be hidden away. AIDS challenges the Church to look again at its attitudes, its attitudes to judgement, to morality and to respectability. The challenge for the Church is to work on itself, to create its own communities where people can learn to move forward and grow with each other. This is the model we use at CARA; and we always make a point of using people with the virus as teachers. We have much to learn from them.

If we can create places where our hopes and fears are integrated into the rest of our life, secure places where people can begin to deal with deep issues then there can come a tremendous sense of spiritual awareness. I think I have learnt more about spirituality from non-Christians than I have from Christians. So much of what Christians seem preoccupied with gets in the way of spirituality. They talk a lot about prayer but seem unable to give any practical help about how to get on and do the thing. But it's more than this; we need to help each other to listen to other people, to see how people feel, to be attentive to the whole person. When we begin to attend to who we are, what we are for and where we are going then spirituality can be brought alive. The tension here for me is that it has been very hard work to discover in my Christianity anything that has helped me to cope with my diagnosis and these important spiritual questions. I discovered that my concept of God was actually useless when it came to the diagnosis, and this caused me a lot of pain.

For seventeen years I was a real kind of 'Jim'll fix it' type of parish priest; you know, you name it and I'll do it. When I went out to San Francisco to work in a hospital chaplaincy suddenly things were stood on their head for me. There were lots and lots of people near death and the first thing they said was, 'Oh no dog collars—we don't need dog collars.' I learnt that this ministry was not about bringing my package of the sacraments to people, but was about just being there, staying with the pain as it really was. It was about the hell of just staying there with no role and nothing to do, no goods to deliver. This was a very powerful transformation for me. I realized how often we ease our own feelings by doing something. We actually make ourselves feel better by saying, 'Let me say a prayer', because I have nothing else to say. I learnt how a lot of traditional patterns of pastoral ministry are actually abusive of people. Working with HIV has taught me a great deal about alternative pastoral care. I think this is about listening instead of giving answers, not offering anything beyond good listening, except when it's specifically obvious that you are able to give something. I think it's helping individuals to feel safe enough to begin to feel who they are, and to be there for that person without any bag of tricks. That means you have got to be very clear about what's going on for you too and that's radical. One has got to know one's own need for support and love, to know one's own feelings are real and it's OK to have them though they may not always be the feelings you want to have. I am excited by all this because I think that if we were to explore an alternative model of ministry the Church would be a very different Church. We could open up all sorts of possibilities. So I believe that HIV and AIDS are teaching the Church many things and I hope that the Church can face this challenge. We need to live with the darkness and to claim the light. To live with death and resurrection, hope and fear. The incarnation has the Calvary experience and the Easter experience and these are all parts of the human existence which everyone has to go through.

6

Order and Chaos: The Church and Sexuality

Jeanette Renouf

Why does the Church find it so difficult to look at sexuality? This is a question that seems to have almost as many answers as those who ask the question. There are answers from biblical, theological, psychological, historical and other perspectives. Each answer contains some truth but still the question is asked. Questions about the relationship of sexuality to religious belief seem to have puzzled people from the earliest days of historical records. This is obviously too broad a question to answer in one short chapter. However, the context of this book is fairly specific. This is a book about people who are HIV positive or have AIDS. To narrow the focus further I approach this as a psychotherapist who has for the past ten years worked within the Anglican Communion. I will then be exploring this question from the perspective of a psychotherapist, currently working within the Church of England, concerned about people with AIDS. I will use a typical psychotherapeutic method of case study and reflection on the case, then draw some conclusions as a result of these reflections. The person of Roger Goodchurch, used in the case study, does not actually exist but is drawn from my clinical and personal experience.

Case Study

Roger Goodchurch is a married man in his mid thirties. He has two children, a son aged ten and a daughter aged seven. Roger works for his father's small manufacturing business and will take over the direction of the business in a few years when his father retires. Roger and his family live in a middle-sized market town in southern England.

The Goodchurches have always attended the parish church and Roger is currently on the PCC. The children attend Sunday School and their mother is one of the teachers. Roger feels comfortable with the traditional liturgy and teachings of his church. He finds the many changes going on in society very disturbing and is grateful for the peace and security his faith offers him. He values knowing that he can depend on the same liturgy and message each Sunday to sustain him through the week. He has fairly clear ideas of what is right and wrong and is sure the world would be a better place if everyone would do what is right. He generally believes that God punishes wrongdoers and blesses those who do right. However, he can also see that sometimes it does not appear to work that way.

Roger's life seems pretty secure and uneventful but in fact he is a very troubled man. He is the eldest of four children, two younger sisters and a 'baby' brother, now aged twenty-two. It is the younger brother, Colin, who is troubling Roger. Two years ago Colin announced to the family that he was gay, a homosexual. Roger was stunned, he couldn't imagine such a thing happening in his family. He was very embarrassed and didn't even share the news with his house group from church. He and Colin have never been very close, with thirteen years between them. Roger felt guilty that somehow he should have spent more time with his younger brother and perhaps this wouldn't have happened. Colin had always been a 'mummy's boy', but then the youngest always is, he thought. What had gone wrong? How could this happen? Roger didn't invite his younger brother to the house any more, he felt it probably wasn't good to have Colin around the children. So for the past two years they had only seen him at holidays when there were large family gatherings. Roger found he could hardly bring himself to talk to Colin even on those occasions.

Roger privately believed sex was largely overrated and responsible for a good many problems in the world: homosexuality, unwed mothers, over-population, rape; to name but a few. He and Jean had both been virgins when they married and their sex life had never been terribly exciting but it had improved after the first few years. It was what he imagined most married couples settled into. He masturbated occasionally and felt guilty about that and always vowed to himself that it wouldn't happen again, but it always did. He didn't understand why he did this but it just confirmed his belief that there was something wrong about sexual desire and it had a life of its own that could easily get out of control. Roger and Jean never talked about their sexual relationship. They really never talked about anything except the children, the house, the car and other day-to-day matters. They had never even discussed their faith and what it meant to each of them. Each said they sometimes felt lonely but couldn't imagine why that would be.

Roger's mother had called him to tell him that Colin was ill with AIDS. After the initial shock Roger comforted his mother and then sat next to the telephone stunned. He had no idea how to make sense of this news. He recalled a sermon that the vicar had preached in which he mentioned AIDS and talked of loving the sinner and condemning the sin. When Roger had mentioned this to Colin however, Colin became very angry and spoke of things like dualism and that his sexuality was an integral part of his personhood, the very essence of his being. Colin had ranted on but Roger really never could understand what he had said that so upset Colin. Deep inside Roger did think this was probably God's way of punishing Colin for his sin of homosexuality. Yet, he still loved his brother, could God's love be less than his, Roger's? He too had sinned, were his sins any less punishable? Perhaps Colin had been born a homosexual, as he said he was; did God create him that way? If so, how could that be wrong? Was it fair to expect Colin to live alone without someone he loved? Roger knew he wouldn't want to live without Jean. Roger felt his whole secure world and all he believed in was falling apart. He didn't know which way to turn or what to believe any more.

Case Reflection

Roger is typical of many people I meet both in and out of the consulting room. He is a sincere, concerned, dedicated Christian. Paradoxically, the secure, unquestioning, rather rigid beliefs that undergird his faith also make it more difficult for him to adapt, or relate, spiritually to a rapidly changing world. This causes him pain and confusion as well as hurt to those he loves. He fears change and nothing in his life has adequately prepared him to understand and adapt to a changing society. In many ways he is defenceless, on an emotional and spiritual level, to cope with the contemporary world. This very defencelessness makes him feel vulnerable and fearful in a world that more and more appears to him chaotic; so he retreats to that which feels safe and familiar.

Roger Goodchurch is probably like many other people, both church attenders and non church attenders. Michael and Norrisey, in their discussion of personality types (*Prayer and Temperament*), state that 40% of the general population and more than 50% of those who attend church are 'very practical, they have a work ethic, with a strong sense of tradition and continuity with the past; and they like order and hierarchy in society'.[1] They further describe such people:

> The great conservators and stabilisers of society . . . suspicious of change . . . they usually opt for the status quo and are conservative in their taste and choices. They are great law and order people . . . they are careful, cautious, thorough, accurate and industrious . . . they are the most conscientious of all the temperaments . . . they represent all the positive qualities of the traditional phlegmatic temperament.[2]

In many ways this is a description of Roger. The Rogers of the world form the backbone of our church membership and of society, they like things to stay in order and stay the same, unchanging. They are willing workers and take responsibility to see that things get done, they keep the operation ticking over. Our churches and society need people like Roger. We rely on them to be just the way they are in order to get things done. These same qualities, however, hinder change especially in the area of understanding human sexuality.

Heije Faber in his book, *Psychology of Religion*, explores the same personality type from the theory of psychoanalysis. He would see this personality type as typical of the second, or anal, phase of human development. Faber draws parallels between this development stage and puritanism. He finds in the anal stage a puritan concern for law and order and dislike of that which is considered 'dirty', messy and disordered, physical or emotionally enjoyable. Faber then links the function of religion and the need for order and defines religion serving as a bulwark against chaos. The puritan valued order in life and society, and religion is to help provide and preserve order. Without order security becomes threatened. Faber identifies what he calls the anal cultural pattern of the Church; preserving society and making the good life possible by removing the threat of chaos.[3]

The case study clearly shows Roger as a person who has a strong sense of tradition and values law and order. He is not an adventurous, creative type. Within his understanding of what is right he tries to do what he feels is best for his family, his church and his community. He likes his life stable, secure, dependable and ordered. His spirituality is one of carefully ordered routine. It is this very routine that gives him the security and inner peace that helps him feel closer to God. It is the very orderliness of his life that is now being threatened. All the things that he values are being challenged, disrupted, threatened by his younger brother's sexuality, his own sexuality and AIDS. These characteristics hinder looking at sexuality realistically.

Roger turned for answers to his church but found that response, like Roger's own, reactive rather then taking constructive initiatives. Roger had been unable to deal creatively and forthrightly with his own sexuality; it is therefore not too surprising that the Church, despite some important movements on certain issues, has not been able to deal creatively and forthrightly with sexuality in virtually any form. Every sexual issue threatens to be divisive and the Church becomes paralysed for fear of fracturing unity. Issues such as homosexuality, the remarriage of divorced persons, the ordination of women to the priesthood, sex education, pornography, wife battering, etc., all tend to be divisive issues that threaten the unity of the Church.

Colin, like many single people, whether homosexual or heterosexual, found himself marginalized by the Church's traditional understandings of sexuality. The Church takes a stand for celibacy in singleness yet many singles do not practice celibacy. To both Colin and Roger it would appear that the Church has condemned all genital sexual expression outside marriage. The Church seems sociologically to be only able to relate to married family units. Yet there are many unmarried, single people who feel the Church is not relating to their situation at all, or poorly. There seems to be an expectation that those who are single will get married and that those who have been married and are now single will simply disappear from the life of the church until they get married again. To many singles, who consider themselves Christian, the Church's position is inadequate and irrelevant to their actual experience of life. For the gay single, like Colin, John McNeill has defined the dilemma thus, 'In order to accept themselves and to affirm their sexuality, they believe that they must leave the Church and even give up their faith; and to affirm their Christian faith, they feel that they must repress and deny their sexuality and lead a life devoid of any sexual intimacy.'[4] The experienced pain and injustice of this dilemma contribute to Colin's anger at Roger and the Church. The Church seems unable to face this dilemma realistically and address it other than in negative terms.

Food, sex and death are three basic reminders of the fragility of being human. Of the three, only sex makes a difference between two sorts of persons, male and female, and therefore penetrates deeper into our personhood. Ever since Colin revealed his sexual orientation Roger has been disturbed at a very deep level. He has been challenged about his own sexuality and his beliefs about what it means to be male and female, to be human. Colin's homosexuality confronted the boundary that Roger believed was there between what is male and what is female and threatened his masculine identity and therefore his identity generally. This threatened boundary was no longer a safe border within which he could rest easy and sure of what and who he was and what he was supposed to be and feel. For twenty years he had been able to relate to Colin secure in his own knowledge that they were both male and of what his understanding of maleness meant. Now he was questioning that whole relationship and his part in it. There was no doubt in Roger's mind that homosexuality was sexual, it was not marriage, it was for pleasure and companionship rather than for duty or procreation. Clearly Colin's sexual orientation was a threat to all Roger regarded as necessary to an ordered social, cultural, and personal identity. Therefore in Roger's thinking, it must be against God. These thoughts, which had always been comforting and reassuring to Roger, became frightening when they were applied to someone he knew and loved.

Conclusion

What can we learn from Roger Goodchurch about why it might be difficult for the Church to look at sexuality?

There are many churchpeople who don't want change, and value the Church when it is unchallenging in morals, ethics and especially sexuality. The traditional stance on sexuality, as well as on other social and political issues, is an important reason why Roger and others like him attend and support their church. To take account of scientific research into the nature of human sexuality, and the social psychological data about men and women in community, families, work, and to consider seriously current psychological insights into what it means to be a sexual person, is to challenge what has come to be accepted as the historical position of the Church with regard to human sexuality. Such a challenge would most likely result in conflicts and cause disunity, pain and change in the life and witness of the Church. For the Rogers of the Church, this is too costly.

Sexuality is of the essence of our personhood and is a reminder of our vulnerability. Sebastian Moore osb observed that

> The reminder that men and women get of their incompleteness by looking at their body sexually is a subtler, deeper, and above all more emotionally involving reminder than that of pangs of hunger and mortality. These three things (food, sex and death) remind us of our cosmic loneliness.[5]

Sexuality has the ability to make us lonely as well as to draw us together. Our sexuality and loneliness draw us into relationship with one another and in such a relationship we become vulnerable to each other. Questions are then raised in each individual: How vulnerable am I willing to be with this person? How close do I want to get? Is it safe to let this person really know me? Out of our loneliness we want connectedness but fear being vulnerable to each other, as we often fear being vulnerable to God. This fear of being known by, and knowing another, becomes evident in the inability of some people to make a commitment, to be vulnerable to another; the inability to sustain interest in a loving relationship; or actively to realize that loving does indeed involve fear and loss, and hurt and death. Roger feared being vulnerable. He was fearful of being vulnerable with both Jean and Colin. He also did not want to be vulnerable in his faith and relationship with God. In all his relationships it was safer to keep them on a somewhat superficial level but Colin forced Roger into a more vulnerable position. Roger was caught in a paradox of wanting a relationship but fearing the vulnerability that would make such a relationship fulfilling. For the Church to honestly and realistically explore issues of sexuality, requires a willingness to be vulnerable, a willingness to be exposed, suffer, and lose control over a dynamic it cannot fully understand or direct.

For the Church to look anew at sexuality is to allow the potential for disorder, disunity, conflict, chaos, and increased anxiety in a time when much in society appears to be out of order. Roger's fears of sexual behaviour running rampant is a mirror of the anxieties of many in the Church. Homosexuality especially challenges what it means to be male and female. AIDS touches primal fears of sexuality and death. With such sensitive and potentially explosive issues at stake it is not difficult to understand that the Church is reluctant to grapple with sexuality and its manifold implications. However, it is for exactly these same reasons that the Colins of the world have a right to expect the Church to address openly this human predicament effected by human sexuality.

Healthy sexual activity, notes Henri Nouwen in *Sexual Dimensions of the Celibate Life*, includes an integration of the sexual and spiritual. Sexuality focuses on embodiment and spirituality accents love. Sex can vitalize, concretize and incarnate love, and love can deepen, transcend and spiritualize sex. People, says Nouwen, who separate sexuality and spirituality therefore are unwhole people.[6] When we find bodily life an embarrassment to our spiritualized religion we lose our capacity for passionate caring and justice. We lose the sense of holiness of the bodies of starving children, and the bodies of women and men torn by violence and torture, and the bodies of people with AIDS. The search for a deeper and more meaningful spirituality on the part of many people involved in the AIDS crisis is a search for connectedness, a reconciliation with God, self and others.

AIDS provides an opportunity for the Church to be what it was intended to be—a witnessing and healing community. It provides an opportunity to heal relationships across boundaries of sexuality, colour, and economics, to explore more fully what healing means, be it healing from the time-bomb of AIDS or from the ever-present nuclear bomb. AIDS provides an opportunity for the Church to be a place where people can share their woundedness, their vulnerability and their search for healing. If Roger can allow himself to be vulnerable to the pain and suffering, joy and opportunities of people with AIDS, to hold his brother's hand, perhaps he will be able to know himself and his God at a new level. To accept the opportunity to respond in love and compassion to the whole sexual person with AIDS is to accept God's mandate to be part of a healing, witnessing and serving community, to heal the broken and oppressed. This requires leaving the pew in order to be present and available to help overcome the barriers and to connect as members of the human family and of Christ's Body, the Church. However, this will require that Roger overcome his fear and open himself to the risk of vulnerability and change.

Finally, then, we return once again to the question, Why does the Church find it so difficult to look at sexuality? The question remains only partially answered. Does the 'why' really make any difference? Does knowing the answer change anything? Whether or not we know the 'why' we are confronted with a here and now situation of pain, hurt, and injustice. A situation in which we Christians are challenged to become fully engaged in light of our understanding of the gospel. As people of faith, we continue to live in the reality of a fallen world with the knowledge that it is not until the last of the oppressed are free that the oppressor will be free and the Reign of God will be more fully present. The real question seems to be, When will we live, open our mouths and speak the gospel language of love, truth and justice as we, as Christians, embrace our brothers and sisters living with AIDS and confront through the power of the Spirit this terrible crisis experienced in all parts of the world?

NOTES

1. C. P. Michael and M. C. Norrissey, *Prayer and Temperament* (Charlottesville, Virginia, The Open Door, Inc., 1984), p. 47.
2. ibid. pp. 47-8.
3. H. Faber, *Psychology of Religion* (Philadelphia, Westminster Press, 1975), p. 219.
4. J. J. McNeill, 'Homosexuality: Challenging the Church to Grow', *The Christian Century*, 11 March 1987, vol. 104, No. 8.
5. S. Moore, 'Sex, God and the Church', in M. A. Huddleston, ed., *Celibate Loving*, (New York, Paulist Press, 1984), p. 153.
6. H. J. Nouwen, *Sexual Dimensions of the Celibate Life*, (Dublin, Gill & Macmillan, 1979), p. 33.

Sebastian

Sebastian Sandys is twenty-seven and lives in the East End of London. He began a theology degree, has lived at Taizé and spent a time as a novice in The Society of St Francis. For the last eighteen months he has been working alongside people with AIDS.

Ten years ago I left home and moved to London. I was seventeen and gay. Life at home had not been unhappy but for the first time I began to find that sense of freedom and liberation that a big city can provide. Ten years earlier at the Stonewall Bar gay men had for the first time fought back against the oppression and bullying that for so long had seemed a necessary part of being gay. The liberation movement was on its way and appeared to many of us, at that time, to be unstoppable. Even the assassination of Harvey Milk in San Francisco served only to provide fresh impetus and give us the determination to assert our right to be free. The love that had not dared to 'speak its name' was suddenly to be heard vociferously proclaiming itself out of the closet and out to stay.

Ten years on I feel cheated. In 1981 something called AIDS gave bigotry and prejudice a new focus, a new excuse. Gay men were a threat again, not simply to 'family life' but now to life itself; and those who declared themselves our opponents did not hesitate to use this new 'plague' to feed the fires of hatred. As gay men we found ourselves faced with the biggest threat to our freedom so far.

In London part of establishing my identity as a gay man was discovering one of those Anglo-Catholic shrines in which, provided I conformed to a particular form of high church campery, wore lace and drank gin, acceptance could be found. It appeared that even in the Church where I had learned that Jesus wanted me for a sunbeam, being gay was not an obstacle in the way of salvation. How naive that has turned out to be. I had hoped that, in the face of disease and oppression from 'outside' the Church would stand up and support us. After all it was gay people who, from where I was standing, filled the pews and paid the bills. But no. In the face of cries of 'the wrath of God' the

Church not only did sweet f.a. but in many cases actually sided with those who were out to destroy us. Gay and straight they marched through the lobbies of Synod declaring us to have fallen short of their heterosexual ideal. They stood silent while the government forced through Section 28 and finally the Bishop of London looked on as our Archdeacon evicted the Lesbian and Gay Christian Movement from our own office. Over the last few years I have discovered just how firm is hypocrisy's grip on the Church of England. And yet I stay. No longer at the centre. No longer an ordinand or in a habit but I do stay.

Polemical I may be, and perhaps it is *too* simplistic to rail against something as unspecified as 'the Church'. When I am less angry I can find the positive and the creative in all of this. There are many examples of courage and compassion that have come from those who call themselves Christian. Some are even beginning to see that people with HIV can teach us all something of how we relate to each other and build community. It is this sense of community that I believe holds the key to how we can all, as 'the Church', face up to and meet the challenges given to us by HIV. It will I believe be through a growing sense of our common life and through a commitment to common prayer that we can together halt the tide of prejudice and rediscover that truth which will set us free.

We need to get it right this time. If we as a body fail to meet this challenge I'm not sure that we will get another chance. As a gay man, I need that sense of togetherness and solidarity with the Church if I am to continue to stay with it. Without this the Church becomes irrelevant to me. If those in the Church who make decisions on my behalf do not stop kicking me in the teeth then I, with so many like me, will refuse to remain marginalized and be forced to exclude ourselves all together. My naive optimism of ten years ago has gone, but in its place has grown a hope, rooted in the common experience of gay Christians, that all is not yet lost and that there is still time to reclaim the gospel for ourselves and together build that community of which I dream.

7

AIDS and the Will of God

Edward Norman

It is often said that men and women in contemporary Western society cannot cope with the fact of death. Actually it is life they cannot cope with. Their expectations relate to personal happiness and to security, neither of which are attainable with the consistency and reliability demanded. Christianity envisages other purposes for human life; it portrays existence as transition across an uneven terrain whose contours allow scale and texture to the individual perspective. Where modern people expect the flat landscape of happiness, religion has always recognized the material realities that in fact provide the heights and depths from which experience derives enrichment. Where complete security is the goal there is no great prospect of advance: religion involves a venture into the hazardous places where, not the body only, but the whole of the human person, is exposed before the mysterious and the ultimate.

The men and women of today seek to domesticate the planet, yet religion calls them to discover that the world and its values have transient qualities. The assault of misfortune, a social dislocation, the turn of warfare, an unfulfilled ambition, the chance contraction of a fearful illness: all these once called forth human nobility, as the individual was tried and tested, and his interior life found to be durable in conditions of adversity. In the modern world misfortune is simply unacceptable, and men attempt to legislate away the ills that afflict them with the same species of unreality that they bring to their hopeless pursuit of happiness.

In the end it comes down to our inability to put up with our status as created beings. We inveigh against an existence in which there are 'disasters'—earthquakes, transportation accidents, illness. Some of these are actually of our own making: we are victims of our own creations, in the sense that our predecessors did not die when an aircraft fell out of the sky, because they had no aircraft. But some of them, and especially illness, seem cruelly built into the structure of the world, and even the most experienced Christian expositors appear agnostic when asked for an explanation of how they fit into the designs of a loving God. It is as if they expect God to act by magic; as if the nature of material reality is to be regarded as satisfactory only so long as it tends to benefit the pursuit of human happiness, but to be regarded as unacceptable when people are themselves seen to be a part of the ordinary material creation, subject to the same laws as everything else.

There are, indeed, no real 'disasters', if we give up describing the planet in terms of what conduces to the contentment of men and women. Humanity cannot be separated from its element: nature. The creation is real and concrete. God set it out with material form and design, and the great gift he gave to men was the capability of self-consciousness—to be able to recognize and to categorize the phenomena of their context. Men were lifted from the programmed unconsciousness of the ephemeral mass of living things and accorded the powers of reason and reflection.

Thus, as the Book of Genesis disclosed in a series of arcane images, men joined with God in the dynamic progression of the world, and used the materials of the creation, including themselves, creatively. They also became discontented as their imagination raised them to expectations of life which transcended their continuing and necessary dependence on their own material constitution. Their vision of happiness and security, that is to say, is ultimately incompatible with their status as creatures. They are still inseparable from the living film that coats the globe and which survives in a condition of permanent mutual absorption: living cells feeding upon one another, in a massive witness to the unity of the creation. Yet people have used their reflective capacities to manipulate this divine scheme, and in joining with God in the development of the planet they have evolved a view of human entitlement to freedom from the material laws of the earth that God did not warrant. So the divine order and the escalating expectations of humanity have come into conflict, and the ills which afflict humanity are now seen by them as evidences that there is no God.

Illness has, of course, no moral value in itself. It is what happens when we are successful hosts to other living things, to collections of cells whose indebtedness to the mechanics of the creation is as authentic as ours. Illness is when the cells of our own body malfunction. It is actually then that we are most truly at one with the rest of creation; allowing life to viruses and bacteria, to cells which grow in the 'wrong' place—wrong, that is, in relation to the requirements of our normal physical functioning. Then we should be most aware of our community with all other living matter, and of the primordial state of things from which God raised us; 'For we know that the whole creation groans and travails in pain together until now' (Romans 8.22).

The biological development of immunological repsonses, the programming of cells to produce shape and structure, the gift of the reflective capacity of intelligence: all have operated to separate out humanity from the rest of the living mass. Released, in some particulars, from the conditions which determine the behaviour of the mass, humanity is outraged when the basic laws of life still turn out to apply. Illness is both natural and normal. Because it threatens our autonomy, and sometimes our continued existence in human shape, we not surprisingly find it unacceptable. We have been able to join with the Creator in advancing medical science, and thus, again, to use the laws of the creation for our benefit. The Lord himself, in his earthly life, offered the great example of curing sickness. The vocation of healing, therefore, is a Christian work, and has always been recognized as such, not only because it shows compassion to the afflicted but because it is mankind as it was called by God to be: a participant in the creative process.

In some societies, and in some cultures, illness has been judged the punishment of personal sin. It is seen as an affliction sent by God. But this is to misunderstand the mechanics of creation, and to envisage a God who operates arbitrarily (for all are sinners but not everybody is visited with sickness) in a series of divine effusions. All of Christian history, it is true, demonstrates examples of cures elicited in response to prayer—miraculous interventions. Why should not illness, in reverse, be employed by God in a comparable miraculous manner? The answer lies in the nature of God's intentions for his people. Everything that Christians know about God indicates that he is concerned with judgement, and with *personal* judgement at that. But the whole nature of creation suggests that this judgement is in the future (where, indeed, Jesus locates it in most of his sayings), and that it rests upon the total experience of individuals in the world. The Bible, certainly, is full of examples of particular nations and peoples being judged by God through historical dramas, in the turn of battle, the affliction of dreadful disease, enforced exile, and so forth. There is a strong case for supposing that God is concerned with collective punishment in the world, and perhaps, even, for 'sending' plagues in order to make particular societies stop in the midst of their material preoccupations or wrong-doing and to ask themselves some deeper questions about their use of the gift of life.

Individual affliction is another matter, however. A plague is a collective description of individual afflictions, but the individuals themselves are plainly not targeted by God; everything that can be known about the nature of the creative processes and the mechanics of life shows that. The explanations men have attached to individual affliction have always derived from highly relative judgements, depending on the sacral values of a society at a given time. The notion that an illness, even a terminal one like AIDS, is a response by God to sexual conduct by an individual—in a world of genocide, social injustice, and unspeakable human cruelties—is ludicrously disproportionate. Why should God punish minor offences (even supposing they really *are* offences) in such a terrifying manner? The answer is that he doesn't. Illness has, for the individual, no moral qualities, and it conveys no moral message. The sins of humanity are pretty evenly distributed, and the whole point about the entry of Christ into the world was the forgiveness of sins. All have sinned and fallen short of the status to which God raised humanity when he imparted the capabilities of reason and reflection, when he called men and women to join with him in the progression of creation, in what we call 'science', and in the cultivation of the planet. Jesus came into the world not to save the righteous but sinners. He did not come to threaten them with horrific illnesses.

It is up to us to determine how we may discover moral and spiritual dimensions to illness. The answer to the humanly inevitable question, 'Why did this happen to me?' should not suggest divine (or other) retribution but incentive to explore the place of men and women in the created order. Just as illness is not the consequence of specific personal sin so the meaning and significance which it portends is not specific to the individual. In sickness and death humanity experiences a common bond: with past generations of living things (whose cellular successors we have carried around in the tissue of our own bodies), as well as with the contemporary world. Consciousness of individual sin, and the desire of contrition, are very central to the message of Christ, who freely offers forgiveness to those who repent. A sense of individual sin may in fact accompany any human misfortune, including illness, but the value derives from the spiritual culture in which the believer is enveloped, not from the cause of the misfortune; and should, anyway, present itself to the Christian in all kinds of circumstance, and not only when our senses are heightened and attuned by life's dislocations. Illness, it must be repeated, is not a catastrophic aberration of the world's order, and should not prompt psychic disorientation. It is a normal accompaniment of our humanity, and points to enhanced submission to the designs of Providence on the one hand and to increased determination to join with God in the divine work of medical science on the other. It is not surprising that men and women today cannot cope with life if they will persist in regarding one of its most normal features as a monstrous cosmic injustice.

Knowledge of illness and its treatment have undergone enormous development over time, especially recent time. Now there is another dimension of the AIDS crisis which should also be developed. Although there is no necessary connection between HIV infection and homosexual conduct, and although it is possible that, through future changes in the nature of the virus itself, the disease may cease to be considered a venereal one, the sad fact is that for the time being, in the perception of the Western countries, AIDS and homosexuality are linked. The persistent public belief that an illness confined to two groups—gays and drug users, both of whom are outside conventional sympathy—is no great threat to society at large is in itself dangerously wrong. It is also dehumanizing. Most people with AIDS at the present time are Africans; the fact that they have been so largely ignored by Western opinion probably rests on a kind of unconscious racism. It is as if observers regard a tragedy to human life as less serious in a black society than in a white one. The liberal conscience of the West is excited by revelations of starvation in African countries, but the far greater threat of AIDS to those people is scarcely considered. Part of the reason for this is the homosexual label attached to AIDS in the Western world. It is as if gays don't matter here, in the way blacks in some distant lands do not. The gay minority is interpreted as having deserved a self-inflicted wound.

This tells us something very appalling about the condition of the moral and human sense of Western societies, and it indicates, furthermore, that the selective conscience of Western men and women is fired by some very durable prejudices. When it comes to moral attitudes to human sexuality the prevailing mood, in even the most secularized minds, remains indebted to the deposit of centuries of Christian teaching.

How Christian is this Christian teaching? The appearance of AIDS in the world gives the Churches the opportunity, which so far they show few signs of taking, to re-examine their theology of human sexuality. Or, to refine the issue in a manner apposite to the present matter, to ask whether homosexual orientation and conduct should be re-valued. If illness as such, has no moral qualities, does homosexual orientation, as such, have none? And what kinds of moral interpretation should be attached to homosexual conduct in the light of modern cultural and medical knowledge about the width and relativity of human sexual behaviour?

The case for a change in Christian attitudes to sexuality is pressing, and examination of it should not be held back by fear of its being difficult to determine what is basic and unchanging. Attempts to isolate and identify the stable content of Christianity are as old as the faith itself. The fact is that, despite appearances established on recent assumptions, there has never been a particularly stable content to Christian teaching on human sexuality, as on many matters of discipline and morality. There has been, instead, a series of adaptations of emphasis according to shifts in the general moral climate. It has been a dialectic: the Church informed society, and social need, for its part, informed the Church. Christ did not entrust his message to philosophy or a rigidly tabulated theory of ideas, but to men and women, 'the people of God'. He founded, not a fixed intellectual system, but a Church. We are the direct successors of those to whom Christian truths were first delivered, and we are charged with handing them on inviolate to our successors. The treasure is, nevertheless, in earthen vessels; the human agency frail and persistently liable to error. However, if we start reinterpreting Christian teaching on sexuality, or anything else, where will it end?

In reality, of course, each generation of Christians has always engaged in just such reinterpretation, and what we are charged to transmit to our successors is already very far removed from the religion which would be recognized by the early Church. Our view, today, of the place of women in society would have been profoundly shocking to the first Christians; so would our attitudes to family life (and especially our rejection of a patriarchal structure), our emphasis on the integrity of the individual over the collective, our disregard of any kind of ritual dietary conventions—and an enormous number of instances of daily life in which a secularized frame of reference has replaced religious observance. Indeed, modern Christians find contemporary societies in which the daily round is linked to religious observances (as in some Islamic states) clearly distasteful, and call them 'fanatical'. Many who now think it right to proceed with the ordination of women to the priesthood must also know that such an arrangement would have horrified most of the Christians who have lived during the past two thousand years. The possibility that sexual acts between gays have also been wrongly condemned for the same length of time will not, if they are consistent, be beyond discussion.

The implicit question is about 'Development', as the present writer pointed out to a Terrence Higgins Trust conference in January 1988. It is to ask how in the modern world we can believe things which were unknown to our predecessors or were rejected by them, and still claim them as authentic aspects of Christianity. Some nineteenth-century scholars, including Cardinals Franzelin and Newman, argued that even *dogmas* of the Church were sometimes unfolded over centuries; beliefs like the Immaculate Conception and the Assumption of the Virgin were examples. For the present purposes, however, it is only *teachings* or applications which are pertinent. The Church has always distinguished carefully between fundamental Christian truth—doctrine or dogma—and its moral and disciplinary teachings. Doctrine is completely stable and describes central tenets of faith. It may be added to over time, as Franzelin and Newman contended, according to some process of 'development', but even then it must be shown that traditional belief had anticipated formal definition by centuries of popular adhesion. Teachings are very different. They are variable and devolved, and because of the evolutionary relationship of Christianity to culture they periodically require adjustment according to circumstance.

Now the work of adjustment and adaptation is a very hazardous enterprise, and people will always dispute amongst themselves about the nature or desirability of particular acts of reinterpretation. But teachings do change, as the human agency of divine truth is dynamic; and we are called to participate in the divine theatre of creation by ourselves becoming activists in the unfolding drama of life on earth.

Questions of human sexuality are matters of teaching and application, not of doctrine or dogma. There are precedents even in the Church of England, whose sense of a doctrine of the Church is not very evident, for adjustments to traditional teaching on sexuality. Perhaps the most radical of these in recent times occurred in 1930, when the bishops at the Lambeth Conference reversed the declaration against artificial methods of birth control given off by the Lambeth Conferences of 1908 and 1920. The declarations of Lambeth Conferences, it is true, do not constitute official church teaching, but they are as near as Anglicanism can get to an expression of its mind. Today, one may presume from the results, many clergy (and doubtless even some bishops) practice contraception. In 1908 their predecessors declared artificial methods of birth control a 'moral evil', whose use would 'deprave'. Are we to assume that the Church's change of mind in 1930 implies that the clergy and the bishops of today are free of depravity? It would be agreeable to think that the reversal of teaching was in line with truth.

How then are we to view the nature of the Church's previous teaching on homosexuality? Many of the sexual practices now considered quite acceptable within heterosexual experience were once also condemned by the Church under various categories, including lust, fornication, and so forth. How is the line to be drawn between these and comparable acts performed between same-sex partners? The original horror of homosexual relations arose in primitive societies in which people were a scarce resource. Taboos surrounded sexual practices which inhibited the procreation of children. With a short life expectancy it was also essential to sacralize the integrity of family units in order to guarantee the survival of children. Today there are too many people, and longevity has imposed unexpected strains upon the marriage bond—which was never expected to last for several decades. The moral discipline surrounding marriage is largely the product of societies in which it must have been relatively unusual for partners to survive more than a couple of decades.

These kinds of changes, whose purpose is laid up by Providence, ought to have some bearing on the adaptation of Christian teaching. Since it is now reasonably clear that homosexuality is not some dreadful perversion of a timeless sexual norm, and does not fall short of any standard that can be shown to be stable, it is surely not, in itself, to be regarded separately from other sexual expressions which celebrate human companionship and love. Many gays are born gay, or are brought up in early circumstances (over which they have no control) which dispose them to homosexuality. Their instincts, that is to say, are put there by God. Are we to suppose, as the General Synod of the Church of England would appear to want us to suppose, that homosexual orientation is morally acceptable but that homosexual practice is not? What sort of God is envisaged, who sends his children into the world with compulsive instincts, which they did not choose, and who then denies them the affection and consolation of shared sexual experience? In all other areas of moral discourse, the modern Church is quite emphatically insistent that it is improper to separate orientation from practice: as seen in the frequent dismissals of 'other-worldly' religion, and in the persistent exhortations to social activism.

Good can come from the chance that AIDS is for the present associated with homosexuality, if it prompts Christians to reconsider. If it is recognized that illness, as such, has no moral imperative, but that its incidence may move us to moral reflection, then Christians ought to be moved to think again about the kind of response AIDS may make them take in regard to their homosexual brothers and sisters. If the names of all the gay saints and doctors of the Church, through the centuries, were to be excised from the calendar many gaps would be left. AIDS has come to the world as a visitor of death, and in this society the first to be called away are those whom society has for long been taught to reject. The double catastrophe will be compounded still more if fear of the illness reinforces ignorant moralizing about homosexuals. People with AIDS themselves offer examples of quiet nobility in suffering—which at times seems to suggest, even to those unable to recognize it, the divine presence. The shadow which now covers human society may precede a fearful darkness to come; the resilience of the Christian life derives, however, from recognizing that the Christ who came into the world to share its experiences with sinners is with sinners still.

Victoria

Victoria is an experienced nurse who has been living with the diagnosis of being HIV positive for the last eleven months. She has had wide experience of caring for people suffering from terminal cancer but finds it hard to see much creative meaning and hope in her situation.

I am fairly sure that I contracted the virus from my last lover Jonathan. We had had a very supportive and loving relationship for eighteen months when he started to suffer from a whole series of illnesses. He told me that he had a brief relationship about four years ago with another man, a Canadian who had been diagnosed with the virus and who had, as a result, contacted all his sexual contacts. I quickly made the decision to be tested and discovered that I too was HIV positive. I don't feel any sense of remorse or guilt about my relationship with Jonathan. Neither Jonathan or myself have been in any way promiscuous. We had both had previous relationships: like many people of my generation I think relationships develop—we form emotional attachments and express our love and commitment in appropriate ways. I don't believe there is anything morally wrong about this pattern of sexual behaviour—I had hoped that one day it would lead to the forming of a lifelong relationship within which I would be able to bring up children.

All those hopes and dreams are now shattered. I found myself caught up in an unfortunate series of connections through which the virus was passed on. In some ways I regret having taken the hasty decision to be tested. It feels to me at the moment that life without the threat of a terminal disease hanging over me would be much more tolerable and hopeful. I am finding it difficult to live in the uncertainty and the fears and anxieties of what life might mean for me in the months and years ahead.

I find it hard to accept all that life has given to me in recent months. I am filled with anger and remorse and, at moments, real despair. It just all seems so terribly unfair and unjust. These feelings aren't just ones of self-pity but are my expression of the sheer sense of horror at what life means for me at this present moment. I am a victim of circumstances over which I have no control. I am victim to a virus that has robbed me of the chance to have children, to continue to grow into a normal sexual relationship through middle age and into retirement. None of these will be mine. I resent it and I am filled with a persistent sense of the utter futility and horror of it all. It hurts.

I find it very hard to listen to people with HIV who are so positive about their experience. I find it very difficult to cope with so many of the people involved in what has been described as the AIDS industry. Who in their right mind would want to surround themselves with so much pain and suffering? Are they escaping from their own? So many AIDS professionals become brokers in others people's experience, controlling it, processing it into languages and meanings and stories that we can share in. I don't mean to sound bitter. All I know in my own life is that I need to face the fact of this virus in all its negativity and life-denying threats. There is nothing hopeful about it. There is nothing good about it. There is nothing positive about it. It is painful, degrading, and fearful. People die horrible deaths. It is hard to measure the amount of human suffering that this virus will inflict upon people.

I don't believe in God in any objective or subjective sense. I have no sense of what God is and have yet to understand how Christians believe God to be active in history. In fact I am rather relieved not to have any religious framework which I am sure would increase the problem of my living with HIV rather than give me any sense of hope. I hope to continue my struggle with this virus; but it must be a struggle that is mine and mine alone. I know that I need meaning and purpose in life; I know that I need to receive love and to give love and I know that I need to have hope and creativity to survive. The threat of death remains, and I continue to live and relive my tremendous sense of grief and loss and pain.

8

Is Health a Gospel Imperative?

Sara Maitland

Early one morning late last summer I kissed my somewhat recalcitrant son goodbye and caught the North London Line from Dalston Junction to Hampstead Heath. It was, like so many mornings that summer, stunningly bright and golden. The pupils of Sainte Union Roman Catholic Girls' Comprehensive were on their way to school wearing their maidenly kilts; from the north St Pancras Station looked even more like a fairy-tale palace than it does coming down the hill from the Angel. The passing mixture of domestic and light industrial buildings of inner north London seemed particularly charming; and flowers as well as brick walls sprouted beside the train tracks.

I was going to the Royal Free Hospital, to be with a friend of mine while he had an HIV test. This was not a panicked response to a passing fear; my friend is well informed and has known and lived with the risks for years. He had decided to have the test now because the US AZT trial results meant that for the first time there was some medical reason for taking the test; there was some hope for prophylactic intervention. In fact for several sensible reasons he rather expected to test positive and we both accepted this probability rationally. He had chosen the Royal Free as one place where he could have the results the same day as the test.

I was touched to have been asked; I was nervous, both of my own reactions and of my ability to meet his needs; I was curious about the whole process. (He told me at one point that it was my capacity for curiosity that had led him originally to ask me for this support; however awful it might turn out to be, I would be one person who would get *something* out of it all.)

Incidentally I would like to say that I was highly impressed by the quality of the care he was offered. It has nothing much to do with this story really, but it is right to give praise where praise is due.

We had about seven hours between when he gave his blood sample and when we were invited to return for the results. We had cream cakes and coffee in the Louis Patisserie. We looked in shop windows and went for a walk on the Heath. We had a long and alcoholic lunch at The

Dôme Café. We bought some books. We wrote a letter to *The Independent* about Neil Kinnock's car smash, and faxed it from a posh little Hampstead stationer's. We talked. Sometimes we talked about why we were there, and sometimes we talked about other things. It was nice, and rare, to have so long together in the sunshine. Once I asked him if he was OK; 'I'll live', he replied, this made us laugh, slightly hysterically. I touched and hugged him slightly more than I usually do. He touched and hugged me slightly less than he usually does.

It was not easy, it was not fun (I'm talking about me now, his feelings are his own) but it was good. I was privileged to be there. More and more throughout the course of the day I admired him: for his clarity about his needs, and his refusal to use them to exploit me; for his openness, self-knowledge and courage; for his self-mockery and his refusal to minimize what was happening. To my love for him, which was strong before, will now always be added a depth of respect, for which I am grateful.

We went back to the hospital at the appointed hour and after a not unreasonable, but unbearable, wait we were summoned to the inner sanctum where he was informed that the test had been negative.

He said afterwards that his first reaction was one of disbelief. Mine was simpler. What I felt was joy, not happiness, or relief, but a great bubble of disinterested, pure joy.

I rejoice and am glad because my friend is well.

I am afraid of Death. Or, more precisely, Death fills me with horror. *Horror: a painful emotion compounded of loathing and fear; a shuddering with terror and repugnance; strong aversion mingled with dread.* OED. This is a very unfashionable thing to say, and is often held to demonstrate neurosis or immaturity, but I seriously believe that anyone who can look at Death without flinching, without any feeling of horror, either has a seriously deficient imagination, or is kidding herself. Whether one believes in annihilation or in judgement—in the complete loss of self, or the complete knowledge of self—death is appalling. In as much as pornography is offensive because it objectifies (makes an object out of) a person, who ought to be a sovereign subject, so much is death the ultimate and final obscenity, pornography. Death, quite brutally, makes an object (a corpse) of a person, and ends subjectivity forever.

Nor, despite all the victory hymns and triumph songs of the New Testament, do its writers ever suggest that death is not horrible: horrible and contrary to the will of the God of life and love. At the death of his friend Jesus wept—wept even as he told Martha that he himself was the resurrection and the life. Confronting his own death,

Jesus sweated blood 'in agony', and prayed to be let off. Death, Paul tells us, is the 'last enemy', the as-yet-undefeated enemy.

This horror is very nearly unbearable, and so it has been wiped away in sentimentality. 'Falling asleep', 'being laid to rest', 'but the gate to life immortal'. Christian iconography has often used lepidoptery as a symbol of death and resurrection: the ugly little caterpillar metamorphosed, through entombment in the chrysalis, into the glorious winged butterfly. Can the caterpillar know, as it spins itself into its tiny shroud, what is about to happen? The chrysalis is not like a womb where a baby grows, nor like a visit to the hairdresser's where you can sip coffee while your physical appendages are restyled. Inside the chrysalis the caterpillar is broken down, disintegrated, reduced to a sort of chaotic ooze—which is then reconstituted. How, I ask myself, during insomniac and lonely nights, how does the caterpillar learn to consent? Learn to face the chaos and the darkness?

Let me be quite clear. It would be nicer to live for ever. Looking the horror in its mean little eye and walking towards it with as much dignity as one can muster simply because there is no other choice, is one thing. Pretending it is a sunny afternoon's picnic is quite another. If death is just child's play there is nothing very redemptive or special in Jesus' passion-and-resurrection conjuring trick.

I rejoice and am glad because my friend is well.

I am afraid of AIDS. Actually I am not afraid of contracting AIDS, although I may of course be proved wrong. I am afraid of my friends contracting it, but I confess that this is not my deepest fear. I am afraid of AIDS metaphorically (and quite separate from a more general fear of life-destroying diseases: in that dimension AIDS seems strongly preferable to, say, motor neuron disease). There can be no question that HIV/AIDS raises very deep fears, and deep fears raise prejudices. AIDS does not just bring us face-to-face with death (bad enough), but with sexuality, and, for me perhaps most frighteningly, it is socially transmitted: we give it to each other in the most intimate moments and ways. (In Freudian terms, which I use only suggestively, rather than diagnostically, there is an extraordinary similarity of imagery in the principle ways in which HIV is transmitted: by sharing needles, by blood transfusion and by sexual activity; all involve penetration and the ejaculation of what should be, and usually are, life-enhancing fluids.) HIV is not random like cancer, nor rat-carried like the plague, but, as the seventeenth-century poet Edmund Waller put it, 'He proffers death who proffers love'. And this, as it happens, is perhaps my own most central fear: that there is an unbreakable and intimate connection between love and death; between passion and violence;

between sex and chaos; between intimacy and destruction of the ego. I am afraid of AIDS because it threatens my real life in the lives of my friends. And still more I am afraid of AIDS because it carries the imaginative delineations of my darkest fears. It is a living metaphor of my own vulnerabilities.

I rejoice and am glad because my friend is well.

And I do not believe that these fears are unique to me. I suspect they are more common than people want to admit. I suspect this in part because they are hard for me to admit.

What do we do when we are frightened?

The first response is usually flight, which socially often presents itself in the forms of denial and repudiation. We *deny* the reality of the fear, we deny that it can touch us, that it has anything to do with us, that it can come within our safe walls of dogma, moralism, sentimentality, self-satisfaction, projection. We *repudiate* any contrary evidence, which usually means the people who are carrying what we fear: we name them as Other, as different from us, as deserving this fearful condition (we don't of course deserve it and so are safe), as invalid witnesses (they're all junkies, foreigners or queers), as anything at all which distances us from our fear: and therefore ultimately as not-persons. This denial and repudiation, decked out as righteousness, has too frequently been the Christian Church's reponse to the incursions of chaos and darkness and is very noticeable at present in relation to HIV/AIDS.

But there are many of us who are too involved, too liberal, too committed to incarnational theology, too self-aware, too generous, too curious (any or all of these and others, alone or in combination) to take flight. There is a temptation then to adopt a second way of dealing with fear: we glamorize it. The word 'glamour' has an interesting etymology: it originally meant magic, enchantment, or spell. Witches 'cast glamour' over a victim. Not until the nineteenth century was it applied to looks, to beauty; and then only in the sense of a magical or fictitious beauty, a delusive or alluring charm.

Partly as a reaction to the denial and repudiation from 'outside', but partly also in response to our own denied fears, it is too easy to dress up people with AIDS in the glamorous robes of sanctification; to clothe them with nobility, to invent the AIDS Martyr, the AIDS Hero.

It is easy, it is alluring, and I believe it is very dangerous.

I have to put my trust in that bubble of joy:

I rejoice and am glad because my friend is well.

It is dangerous because it implies something which if it were true would contradict other truths which seem to me necessary to life and love and wholeness. You can only valorize AIDS if you make a tiny self-contained AIDS universe with different natural and emotional laws from those outside. If, in fact, you marginalize AIDS in precisely the same way as the 'denial and repudiation' approach wishes to.

This glamorization of a specific illness is not new. Epilepsy, for example, has been treated in much the same way within some shamanistic cults. The fear of the Other, of the strange and it must be said disturbing symptoms of epilepsy, could be contained by believing that they were the marks of the gods. The shaman is not like us, the shaman is special, exalted, and used. The shaman and the epilepsy become confused and identified.

It is worth noticing that HIV/AIDS is structurally very amenable to such a reading: it is a mysterious virus (it gets less mysterious every day, but it is still imaginatively mysterious, and the popular media language used to describe it does not help). It sneaks about in the whole bloodstream, not like cancer where you can locate, and often even cut out, the tumour, leaving the person intact. It is extremely difficult to describe in non-scientific language. It produces its symptoms randomly, both in type and time, not following a nice clear path from diagnosis onwards. It is incurable. It is therefore easy for the person and the illness to become confused—and then to exclude the person, either by exclusion, or by glamorization.

I think this is happening sometimes with AIDS, indeed I hear something of this when I listen to myself and to others. I hear an odd tender pride in my own voice if I have been to visit someone in hospital with AIDS symptoms. It is not just, 'Look-how-liberal-a-vicar's-wife-I-am, I know people with AIDS' (though that too to my shame), it is also a vicarious contact with someone who can claim to be in contact, in touch with the most sacred mysteries, who has secret gifts and carries hidden treasures. One of the things my friend and I talked about that sunny day was the 'power' that he felt he had to surrender first by getting the test at all and secondly by getting a negative result: he was by definition excluded from a particular community and therefore excluded from access to particular truths.

But this view of AIDS is only possible if we allow, give credence to, the view that any illness can be God-given. People who deal with their fear by denial and repudiation think that illness can be God-given as a punishment; the flip-side of this coin is to believe it can be given as a grace.

I sat this summer beside my daughter's bed after she had had major spinal surgery. And I *know* with a deep certainty that illness cannot be the will of God. God does not punish our sins by giving us terminal disease; and equally God does not use disease as a sort of training tool. If we should not 'do evil that good may come of it' then we can be quite certain that God *does not* do so. I do not know, I do not understand, why suffering exists in the world, but I am quite clear that it is not a bright idea, a nifty notion, on the part of God to make us shape up; to give us opportunities for self-reflection, for growth, or for moral superiority. It is always a curse that seeks healing, not a blessing. (This is not to say that we may not use the illness positively, that we may not use it as a point of growth and so become humbler, braver, more loving, more conscious; but we cannot claim that this is its purpose, if we want also to hold out for a kenotic God 'who so loves the world' that we are free in it to love each other and ourselves.) The gospel accounts of Jesus' ethics in relation to many forms of suffering are complex, but his response to illness is extremely straightforward: he heals. Not only does he heal but, with the possible exception of his bantering with the Syro-Phoenician woman, he does so promptly and without question.

> 'If you will', says the leper, 'you can make me clean.' And he [Jesus] stretched out his hand and touched him saying, 'I will; be clean.' And immediately his leprosy was cleansed. (Matthew 8.2-3 etc.)

God desires the wholeness and health of all the creation. That is God's purpose in creating it. That is God's purpose in redeeming it. And if not then there is *nothing* worth knowing or doing.

It worries me that we should glamorize any illness to comfort ourselves in our fearfulness. For one thing it leads to lies. The lies become embedded in our language and then it becomes harder to speak the truth at all.

Why, for instance, should it be so unacceptable to use the words 'suffering' or 'victim' in the AIDS arena?

It is the nature of illness that you suffer from it. If you do not suffer there is no illness: that is what an illness *is*. Likewise if you are oppressed you suffer: if you do not suffer you are not oppressed. You can love and know yourself loved without shame, and with self-knowledge, and good humour; you can accept the course of your life with courage and autonomy, but illness and rejection both *hurt*. They cause you to suffer. Attitudes to suffering can vary and change, but suffering itself is there; it is no more a moral issue than the colour of your hair. Most people with AIDS suffer very much; that is why it is an important issue. That suffering cries out for relief, at every level. Certainly if there is no suffering it is entirely unreasonable to expect people to give money to AIDS charities, or to waste their time trying to understand their own fears and prejudices.

Suffering however is not at all glamorous. We do not want our shamans, our priests to suffer; we want them to be above that and show us the way to be above it ourselves. Of course it is tempting to censor the word and try to ban the reality, or at least any expression of it. Unfortunately it is dishonest, and because it is dishonest it is dangerous.

The use of the word 'victim' is far more complicated.

Some of the negative connotations of the word victim, come of course from way outside the HIV/AIDS community; they come indeed from the Church and from a confused Christology. The word victim (which had practically no currency in English before the seventeenth century) originally meant simply a sacrificial animal. Thence it became attached very directly to Christ as our sacrifice: the Paschal Lamb, 'like a lamb to the slaughter', etc. With a deft little jiggle of Christian appropriation of the Hebrew Scriptures we are offered Abraham's sacrifice of Isaac as a typological prefiguring of the sacrifice of Christ. But this depends on an extremely patriarchal understanding of the Trinity, of God. It depends also on defining sonship as infantility, younger-than-ness. In fact one of the interesting aspects of naming God through parental relationships is that the names are mutually inclusive and simultaneous. Those who require that God be *primarily* Parent are at least acknowledging the interdependence of the Trinity, since no one can be a parent until they have a child: there is no father without the son. Isaac really is treated as animal, as completely passive. Abraham lies to his wife and servants about his plans, he deceives the poor child, and prepares to kill him. Not surprisingly then a handy ram is a completely satisfactory substitute. But the First Person of the Trinity does not offer the passive, ignorant and deceived Second Person of the Trinity. Christ offers himself, with knowledge, in the divine will which is his own will, and no substitute is therefore possible. The sacrifice of Christ only has meaning in the understanding that he is both priest and victim; not one or the other. Since nobody can properly *will* (in the sense of choose) AIDS (illness being contrary to the will of God), and since in any case the sacrifice of Christ is 'full, perfect and sufficient' it is clear that people with AIDS are right not to see themselves as victims in this technical sense.

It is equally clear that in a quite different sense of the word people like to ascribe victim status to others, because it deprives those others of autonomy: once they are victim, they are objects of pity rather than subjects of their own humanity: 'A victim is a person who has been deprived of the basic human right to be of service to others.' Since they do not have this right they must accept such definitions as the namers choose to lay on them.

Obviously people must struggle against such objectification, for themselves and for others. The question is really whether that struggle is best engaged by denying the use of a word, or openly challenging its negative connotations. Surely there is a simpler meaning to the word victim? And one that properly handled actually describes HIV/AIDS in the way we would like to understand it—'bloody bad luck'. It is quite acceptable to describe people as 'victims' of an external force: famine, earthquakes, even war, for example. I would want to argue that all illness (far more than war) falls into this category. Because illness has its existence inside us, within our bodies, our selves, where we would like to claim control, we are very reluctant to see it as an external force of devastation. But surely this is what illness, all illness, actually is. Without fault, without volition, without choice some people are subjected by illness to suffering. They are indeed the victims of circumstances. Whether we allow other people to define how we ought then to behave is a completely separate matter.

This does feel important, for if there is no fault, no suffering and no victimization, wherein lies the claim to 'marginalization' which has become a central definition within the progressive theological movement's concern with AIDS? I struggle to stand in solidarity with, and to work on my own bits of, issues around AIDS, because somewhere I do accept the claim of marginalization. The way we are able to respond to, identify ourselves with, embody God's bias towards, the marginalized (the 'poor', the *anawim*) is the way in which we, the Christian community, will incarnate our truth. But if there is neither suffering nor victimization within that community then the claim (implicitly and explicitly made) that the HIV and AIDS community has a particular and demanding 'marginality' looks somewhat bogus. Without the specific elements of suffering and victimization we would be obliged to say that AIDS had actually *reduced* the marginalization (as normally understood) of both male homosexuals and drug users: less silence, more media coverage, more money from both government and the voluntary sector, more attempts, at least, to understand and to listen, than have ever gone into either of these communities before.

The comforts of glamorization are fairly obvious. So too should its dangers be. The danger of creating closed cultic communities in which only those with the highly dubious 'privilege' of HIV positive can represent the priestly casts; in which the language is censored and distorted to allow a curious and exclusive view of the world. A community that uses the discourses of spirituality and liberation for internal self-fulfilment, rather than for political and material action on behalf of all. A community which is necessarily apolitical and self-

100 Embracing the Chaos

absorbed. A community that is Palagian in its attitude to grace, but Epicurean in its attitude to sin.

I do not like writing this article. I want to be righteously non-judgemental, I want to be loved. I am frightened of death and I am frightened of AIDS. I seek every cheap way out of my fears that I can find. But I also believe we must hold on, at whatever cost of comfort, to a concept of a God who made the world for delight, and who therefore cannot and will not consent to the glamorizing of any illness. We need this God, who for love and joy has proven the willingness to face suffering and death, especially in a community which faces the darkness of suffering and death. We need that God even more than we need the delusionary comforts of cultic glamour.

I continue to trust my own joy; I rejoice and am glad because my friend is well. It is only by doing so, by insisting on the primary rightness and goodness of health, that I can also rejoice and be glad because my friends are honest and courageous and walk where they must with their eyes and their hearts open.

Anna

Anna is, perhaps, an unlikely person to have HIV: an attractive middle-aged woman, married with two grown-up children; doing some paid and voluntary work and preparing to take up a new stage in her life. In August 1988 she learnt that her husband had AIDS. Then followed several weeks' shock and pain before she took the test and discovered that she was HIV positive.

Following my test I was helped to take responsibility for my feelings instead of just blaming my husband. Helped by John Shine (then of London Lighthouse) I externalized my emotions. I cried, screamed away the fear and bashed on telephone directories to get rid of the anger rather than doing it on other people. This helped me to keep buoyant, energetic and determined, able to think clearly and make decisions. Without this and counselling help I have no doubt that I would have been mentally ill.

I felt strongly from the start that I didn't want anyone siding with me against my husband because I could see that that wasn't going to help anybody, least of all me. Blaming him would have sidetracked me from dealing with my own situation and wasted time and energy. My hope for a better life depended on learning from my situation; trying to understand how the way I had lived had led me to where I was. Although we have yet to understand why some people pick up the virus after one 'go' and others have numerous sexual encounters and don't, I feel that at some unconscious level I knew I needed to change. I feel that this virus was the catalyst I chose. So although I am very unsteady at the moment as a result of major changes in my life it has been perhaps one of the best things that ever happened to me. It's given me a chance to write, to make new friends, to make my own life, and not to spend all my energy supporting my husband. For the first time in my life I am putting myself first: a feeling that God perhaps has given me another chance. I have felt happy for the first time in my life—a happiness within myself which I have needed to work at establishing. I feel I have embarked on a new and worthwhile life. I know I am going to die some day but that doesn't worry me, at the moment I am absolutely determined that I am not going to die of AIDS and that I am going to have some kind of worthwhile living before death comes.

I have tried all my life to understand God. It seems to me that God is within us and without is *everything*, a disembodied intelligence rather than an old man who sits in judgement thinking, Shall I give the world a dose of AIDS as punishment, or shall I spare them?

One of the things that makes the Church extremely unattractive for me is its attitude to sexual sin: as if flesh should be whacked into submission or it will overpower us and we will descend into utter chaos. We English people are so fearful of physicality. For example, if you go on holiday abroad and you see various nationalities on the beach you can all spot the English person because they carry their body as if it is an embarrassment. (The Church prefers to bury our bodies under mountains of clothes.)

I continue to feel and delight in a sense of freedom to be myself in a way that I have never felt before. I have learnt so many fascinating things about illness: how the mind and body behaves, how to be more 'right-brained', less ruled by rationality. Above all, I am grateful that my own response—to fight—has found such wonderful allies in professionals, family and friends. I have a future. You do not have to die of AIDS.

9

In a Biblical Perspective

Leslie Houlden

AIDS raises no new theological problems. All are as old as the hills, though we feel them with special keenness, as we always do in situations that are both novel and heart-breaking. Because we ourselves have never trodden a path anything like this before, it might as well be that there has never been any such path.

Different cases raise different problems. Those who find themselves HIV positive from the womb can range themselves with Job. They can plead total innocence. They are simply victims of aberrations in the structures of secondary causes, like the victims of hurricanes and avalanches. If God lets those causes run, then no moral questions arise, though one might complain about the total system while being at a loss to imagine an alternative. A resolute Augustinian, it is true, would silence the pleas of innocence, even in cases like these: to be human after the fall is to deserve condemnation and not to be condemned is purest grace. But pitching the matter in terms of justice like this does not now win many hearts. It is a doctrine which would reduce Job himself to an even more abject silence than that brought about by God's overwhelming majesty, as in the book. But it has the merit of placing us all firmly in the same boat, which is where we belong.

In most cases of AIDS, however, the question of deserts comes into the picture from the start; or at least it proves very hard to ignore it. Yet it is hard to bring it in satisfactorily. Leaving aside the matter of causation in the universe and supposing we limit ourselves to thinking in terms of conduct eliciting punishment, we are bound to find the situation extraordinary. The 'punishment' falls randomly, arbitrarily, and with strange concentration on a single offence; as if God were like a chief constable who goes all out for pick-pockets but leaves the burglars aburgling and the pimps apimping with impunity. The Augustinian doctrine of punishment universally deserved makes much more sense that this. It is ironic that some of those who focus on AIDS as specific punishment for specific sin show themselves less than faithful to the Augustinian tradition which has been so formative in their Protestant heritage.

The problem resolves itself into yet another dramatic instance of random, disproportionate suffering. In Judaism and Christianity the classical responses to that phenomenon are akin to each other. They are the story of the *aqedah* (Isaac's 'binding' for sacrificial death narrowly averted) and the crucifixion of Jesus. In the former case, we focus on the story of a putative event; but the aspect of it as event is dispensable, it is the story that matters and invites ever more fathoming. In the latter case, we focus on the event (this happened to Jesus), and the story serves to preserve the memory of it and to interpret it. The two are so far akin that the former is part of the interpretation of the latter from the earliest level of that interpretation. Paul uses its wording in Romans 8.32, and it leaves its mark elsewhere in the New Testament.

The kinship between the two episodes consists overridingly of a single principle. It is that significant good comes by the skin of one's teeth—and it is to be noted that that expression is derived from Job (19.20). It is of course a matter of the deepest offence, inconvenience and even outrage that this principle should be so essential to the achieving of good. One could hope for smooth progress towards that goal, a journey of gradually evolving attainment, and one can point to lives of that kind. But the good reached by that path often lacks maturity of understanding and may be under-appreciated. It has been gained without going through the mill.

This principle is often referred to by Christians as that of death and resurrection, and, because of Jesus, tied specifically to Christianity. But that severs the important link with Judaism; moreover, it is easily misunderstood when put in those terms. For it is not that resurrection follows death in the way that day follows night, simply a matter of sequence and of dependability. It is rather that without death there is not a chance of resurrection; without destruction not a chance of salvation; without painful adolescence not a chance of worthwhile adulthood; without loss of innocence not a chance of sanctity (cf. John 12.24). Let us stick to the principle of good attained by the skin of one's teeth.

A man told of the worst ten weeks of his life. They were spent in mental breakdown, a time of catastrophe and constant pain, of collapse of family and framework of life. It was unmitigated evil at the time. Yet he counted this period as the source of all his good. All he had come to understand stemmed from the experience, all his selfhood, his poise and his manageable hopes. That it should be so was in no way predictable or automatic. It could not be reckoned on, and the good might never have been gained at all. It was good reached by the skin of his teeth, grace hanging by a thread—though also abundant and, once known, overwhelming and certain.

Now if this is the principle for interpreting the disastrous elements and episodes in our lives (and of course we may ignore it or find it incredible, so that disaster becomes a terminus), then it bypasses the scheme which works in terms of justice—that which might be expected of God and the deserts which we incur. On reflection, 'bypasses' is not the best word, for it suggests that the 'justice' scheme is adequate and remains in place, but we manage to steer round it, choosing a more promising route. So perhaps the effect of our principle is rather to transcend or (if that should seem too detached) to subvert and undermine the justice scheme.

It is at this point that the New Testament appears to protest. Is not Paul in particular, the earliest interpreter of Jesus' career and achievement, full of the language of justice? Yes, but he himself adopts it only to subvert it. In Jesus he discerns the one in relation to whom God 'acquits' the ungodly (Romans 4.5), acting in a way that shatters the system of deserts as the mode of God's dealings with us. There have been interminable attempts to save Paul for the cause of God's justice in the familiar sense of his essential equity. But it is not this that concerns Paul: the language is used only to be destroyed. To acquit the guilty is to subvert justice. Such statements are followed not by sober full stops but by exclamation marks. The principle God uses is not justice, but salvation by the skin of one's teeth. How else can we understand Paul's view of the whole sweep of history: 'For God has consigned all men to disobedience, that he may have mercy upon all' (Romans 11.32)? Justice makes no sense of that, but cries aloud in outrage. The one who has reached great good by the skin of his or her teeth knows what it means.

The principle is clear enough in the story of Isaac told in Genesis 22. Is it so clear in the story of Jesus' death? It is very clear in the first telling of that story in the Gospel of Mark. There Jesus' death is, for him, unmitigated catastrophe, as his final words (15.34) make clear (or, if they mean something else, they do not make that clear!): 'My God, my God, why hast thou forsaken me?' Almost unmitigated are the hostility and incomprehension with which Jesus is surrounded—rejected by Jewish leaders, Roman governor and his own disciples. Only certain individuals press through to gestures of faith: the woman who anoints him beforehand for his burial, Simon who carries the cross (which, in the metaphorical sense of the term, 8.34, the disciples wholly fail to do), and the centurion–executioner himself (14.3-9; 15.21,39). They foreshadow the full flowering of good which remains obscured to the very end; for if it is too much to say that the resurrection is only hinted at in this Gospel, it is certainly not described or celebrated. To do that would run the risk of turning the cross into a wrong soon mended. Good is achieved not by natural progression but by the skin of the teeth. We are left in no doubt that there exists no other way through, neither for Jesus nor for those who are attached to him. It is the principle enjoined on his followers (in vain, 8.34; 10.35–45), and implicit in the experience of those disabled ones whom Jesus brings out of personal disaster to follow him 'in the way' (e.g. 10.46-52).

Mark gives no hint in all this of seeing any difficulty in relation to considerations of deserts. Nobody is assessed on grounds of merit, nor is the situation as a whole interpreted along such lines. Rather, especially as far as Jesus is concerned, his story flies in the face of the structures of justice; not in order to scorn them, but in order to undermine them in favour of a different order of things, that of good reached by the skin of one's teeth.

Whether Mark intended to convey all this is uncertain; he is beyond the scope of our interrogation. It is certainly the impression he has conveyed to many of his modern readers who have allowed themselves to be gripped by the flow and the shape of his narrative. There is some evidence that he conveyed it too to some of his earliest readers. At any rate, the writers of the Gospels of Matthew and Luke, who both used Mark as their source, modified him as they used him, in such a way as to make the story of Jesus' death more comfortable at precisely the points where, in Mark, it is demanding and painful. In particular, the natural human concern for merits and demerits, for assessing responsibility and making sure it is shouldered, reasserts itself. None of us should be surprised that it was hard to preserve pure and unsullied the sense that salvation is by the skin of your teeth. It has generally remained a difficult belief to maintain, in Christianity as in ordinary life. Even those of us who are acutely aware of it in relation to ourselves, and even tell our story to others rather proudly in terms of it, scarcely preserve it when we judge other people.

So Matthew, for example, interrupts Mark's story of Jesus' death, as he, largely, reproduces it, to describe (with satisfaction?) the just end of Judas (Matthew 27.3-10). He also makes clear both Pilate's declared innocence of the sentence passed on Jesus and the Jews' acceptance of responsibility for it (27.24–5). Conversely, in 28.16–20, after the resurrection, the disciples are rehabilitated to such an extent that we almost forget their terrifying weakness only a few pages earlier. Their pain, such as it was, was but for a moment, and their future is triumphantly assured. People are morally black or white, wicked or good, chosen for condemnation or salvation. Here one has moved into a world where moral blackness and whiteness are without too much difficulty identified with colour of skin, or comparable straightforward measures of assessment. People get their deserts, and that is wholly proper. Pharisees are wholly unlike Christians.

Luke goes further in showing Jesus' disciples as virtually 'evolving' into what is for Luke the condition of 'the good'—that of successful leadership of the mission in the name of Jesus. They reach it not without incident but with their essential virtue hardly impaired: if they fall asleep in Gethsemane, it is not callously as in Mark but 'out of grief'; if Judas betrays and Peter denies, it is because they are 'got at' by Satan (22.3, 31-4), and in the case of Peter it is but a temporary lapse. They are saved as if by having received a kind of immunity from Jesus, by virtue of his call, not by going through such depths that they are all but lost. Also, the resurrection of Jesus virtually 'evolves', in this telling of it, out of his death. Good Friday holds the promise of Easter, and we need never really worry.

In turning to the story of Jesus' death in the Gospel of John, there is ample room for uncertainty concerning his position on this matter. In a nutshell, it turns on the force to be given to the word 'flesh' in 1.14. When Jesus, the Word, 'became flesh', are we to understand an uncompromising assertion of his human reality, as the sphere wherein the heavenly one now lives, or are we to see a reference to a kind of instrument which the heavenly one uses for his purpose? In the account of his death, there are signs of the latter: it is a voluntary death, not one snatched or imposed (10.18; 13.37); it is a composed, triumphant death ('It is completed', 19.30), far from the anguish of Mark and more like the gentle piety of Luke's, 'Father, into thy hands I commend my spirit' (Luke 23.46). So for Jesus himself the element of crisis is, as it were, subsumed under the mantle of his divine status. The death was so greatly 'glorious' that the resurrection could scarcely add glory. Similarly, the prayer of chapter 17 weaves verbally a protective web around his followers: whatever evil may happen, they will certainly come through, not by the skin of their teeth, but in full armour. As for the Jews, their deep wickedness, irrevocable and incurable, emerges clearly in 8.37-59.

The key to this development in the interpretation of Jesus' death, and of the position of those involved in it, lies partly in the increasing need of the churches of the later first century to understand their own past, and elements of their contemporary scene (e.g. Jewish antagonists), in a way that was clear-cut, justificatory, and reassuring. A profound belief in the common features of humankind is an easy casualty before the pressures of such institutional considerations. 'The other' ceases to be elements within us from which we need deliverance and which we must overcome to reach that good which is only attainable by the skin of our teeth; it becomes 'the other lot', now depersonalized and generalized, those whose plain wickedness lets us off, so that we may progress smoothly towards our perfection and see ourselves as already assured of it.

All this is a great deal wider than the AIDS crisis, but, as this book shows, there are those who have found its truth by way of this example of devastation. It is hard to confine oneself to the essential questions, but emergencies have that effect. The underlying message of the New Testament is that the emergency is now, for us all.

10

What sort of world? What sort of God?

Peter Baelz

> . . . We are beginning to see
> now it is matter is the scaffolding
> of spirit; that the poem emerges
> from morphemes and phonemes; that
> as form in sculpture is the prisoner
> of the hard rock, so in everyday life
> it is the plain facts and natural happenings
> that conceal God and reveal him to us
> little by little under the mind's tooling.[1]

The editor invited me to write a kind of theological postscript to his collection of individual experiences and reflections. Perhaps I should have refused. I could be said to be the odd person out. I was not one of the original group of contributors who met together, talked, listened, agonized, argued, expostulated, pondered, and then put on paper the thoughts which arose most clearly and urgently from their encounters. Nor should I wish, if I could, to act in some quasi-judicial way, sorting out and assessing from an allegedly impartial point of view the various and sometimes contradictory things they have said. Even if the passion and immediacy of experience and response are reflected, for better or worse, in their theological comments, it is vitally important that the rest of us should stop, listen and hear what they are saying rather than hasten to provide what we may like to think is a more balanced and dispassionate judgement. I should greatly regret it if anything I were to add by way of 'postscript' should detract from the full impact of what had gone before.

Our primary concern must surely be practical and pastoral. How may we help and minister to one another in the face of a death-dealing disease of epidemic proportions for which there is as yet no known cure? This concern should engage the hearts and minds of all who profess and call themselves Christians, both as individuals and as members of the Church, not least because the 'institutional' Church is seen by the majority of those suffering from the AIDS virus as having little or nothing to offer them in their time of need by way of understanding, compassion and hope. No doubt the 'institutional' Church could point to certain contributions it has made. There have been churches and congregations, especially in the USA, whose response has been warmly welcomed by the AIDS communities. Even so, we must recognize the fact that, in general, the response of 'the Church' has been perceived to be fearful, judgemental, condemnatory and exclusive.

It is little wonder that such attitudes are described and rejected as 'moralistic'. Those suffering from the AIDS virus are not helped by being told that they have brought the trouble on themselves, that it is their own fault and it serves them right. Here is an emergency which concerns us all. Whatever the causes of the disease—and originally it came as a bolt from the blue—those suffering from it need above all to be affirmed in their humanity, given practical assistance and support, treated with both justice and compassion, and encouraged to find resources for 'life' in the presence of death. In short, their fundamental and pre-eminent need is to be 'accepted' as members of the community, not rejected as pariahs. And is not the grace of God, which Christians proclaim, a grace of acceptance, not of condemnation?

Here, perhaps, a word of caution might be in place, one that needs to be taken on board some other time. It is indeed true, so Christians believe, that God accepts us as we are. But it is not the whole truth of our salvation. Certainly his love does not wait upon our deserts. He meets and accompanies us in our time of need. But his love does not leave us as we are. It challenges us to become what, as his creatures and under his providence, we have it in us to be. His love is a demanding as well as a compassionate love, such as we can discern in the teaching and life of Jesus.

> The demand was not diminished or contradicted by the compassion. On the contrary, it was because the demand was of such extreme clarity that compassion, genuine engagement and sympathy, could arise from it; for the demand places a value on people, and on what their lives are worth, which cannot arise in any other way. These two, demand and compassion, which might so easily have existed in a hopeless and impossible tension, were held together in the word and in the activity of 'forgiveness', that with God nothing is impossible since his nature is now disclosed as love.[2]

Though 'moralism' is to be eschewed, since it perverts the gospel of grace into a sentence of condemnation, nevertheless moral considerations have, in their proper time and place, to be taken into account. This is not a backward-looking matter of deciding who is to be blamed for what. We all need a deeper sense of shared responsibility without shelving a corresponding sense of individual repsonsibility. Rather it is a forward-looking matter of deciding what, in the fulfilment of our God-given humanity, we are, singly and together, being called to become. What, for example, are we to say about the drug-culture as such? Most people would conclude that this does not offer a fulfilment of our true humanity. Or what, again, are we to say about our sexuality, in all its varied individual, social and institutional aspects? Certainly there needs to be another look at the 'theology of sexuality' and the 'carnality of grace' in terms of God's 'Yes' to our basic nature as bodily and sexual beings. Flesh and sex are constituent features of our createdness. And certainly developments in psychology and in the practice of contraception should be taken into account in reconsidering an appropriate Christian moral response. But sex has a vast potential for both good and ill, and we shall still need to work out what significance we believe should be given to our sexual relationships in terms of pleasure, love, commitment, fidelity and procreation. And we have to recognize the fact that in this delicate and complex area equally sensitive and responsive persons come to different conclusions and the Church is not yet of a common mind.

Inevitably the AIDS crisis raises fundamental questions of attitude and orientation. When death is imminent, life takes on new significance. The institutional Church, it seems, too readily recoils in ignorance and fear from the threat of AIDS. It is those infected with the AIDS virus themselves who discover among their own number the possibility and reality of compassion, caring, interdependence and hope. Through their shared weakness they find new strength, through their sense of despair new hope. It is as if they, rather than the institutional Church, are the ones who bear witness to the reality of 'resurrection from the dead' or 'salvation by the skin of one's teeth'.

It is not surprising, then, if the structures of the Church are rejected in favour of a community of the spirit, preservation in favour of vulnerability, order in favour of disorder. Nor is there any need to deny that the Spirit of God is indeed present amidst the chaos and confusion, breaking forth in new and unlikely places, anywhere and everywhere carrying out his anonymous and life-giving work. God's kingdom is deeper and broader than the visible Church. The Spirit of life and love is not limited to its structures, or even to its sacraments.

Might there, nevertheless, be some risk that out of this new experience, and in the face of misunderstanding and rejection, a new onesidedness may unwittingly and unintentionally be born? Psychologically, it is difficult, if not impossible, for most of us to live in a continual state of crisis, or, to change the metaphor, to stay on the mountain-top. After two years in hospital, when once again I saw a red letter-box, it was aflame with the glory of God. Now it is no longer so. I recall the experience, but it no longer overwhelms me with its original immediacy and power. On a more profound note, one of the problems of the early Church was to rediscover the significance of the gospel when the world continued along its course and the expected coming of the kingdom of God was again and again delayed. Somehow or other the vision of the mountain-top has to be remembered and re-expressed in the often humdrum routines of life in the valley.

There is in human life—indeed there cannot but be—a dialectic between spirit and structure, creativity and order, person and institution. We need to look again at what we may properly hope for from individual persons and what from institutions. The weaknesses of institutions are obvious. Their strengths—of a different kind—are perhaps not so obvious. As 'persons' we need both one-to-one relationships and frameworks in which these relationships may be nurtured and transmitted from generation to generation. The suggestion[3] that, theologically speaking, institutional life belongs to the Old Covenant, while personal relationships belong to the New, is well worth following up. If it is on the right lines, we shall have to consider just how Old and New Covenants belong together, the New transforming rather than abolishing the Old, and both contributing to the fullness of human life.

Something similar may be said about the relation between order and disorder. It is in the interplay between the two that life proceeds. Just as spirit and structure are interdependent, so are order and disorder. It is true that order tends to ossification and that the prevailing human temptation is to hold on to what one already has. Herein lies the way of death. What ceases to change ceases to live. Nevertheless change is sporadic and experimental. If it is to contribute to the fullness of life, it needs, sooner or later, to be expressed and channelled through some ordered continuity.

With thoughts such as these in mind I want now to broaden the context of the discussion and ask two very general questions: What sort of world is it in which we live? and, What sort of God is it in whom we put our trust and hope? These may seem highly 'theoretical' and practically useless questions to be raising in this context. They are questions, however, which cannot ultimately be avoided, especially if we believe that 'the Church is what man is and does when he recognises what is happening in the being of the universe.'[4] In fact they are already present whenever there is mention—as in the preceding pages there has been frequent mention—of the 'vulnerability of God'.

To my mind the question has never been so sharply and poignantly put as it was by Austin Farrer:

> God has made the world, but he has made it (for our purposes) so cruelly, that we appeal to him, to save us from its evils. . . The Rock on which we

hope to stand is the ground and principle of all being. Were he anything less than this, he would be threatened by the transience of created things, and could provide us no ultimate refuge. But then again—here is the paradox—if the God who saves us is the author of nature, then the evil from which he saves us is part and parcel of the nature he has made. . . When we appeal to the God of nature, is it not against the God of nature that we make our appeal?[5]

Consequently, in our present context of AIDS, I wish, with all due hesitancy, to raise these ultimate questions: What sort of world? What sort of God? It is hardly surprising that the Church's first 'official' heretic, Marcion, was unable to reconcile the Creator God of the Old Testament with the Redeemer God of the New.

If we turn to what some contemporary scientists are saying, whether physicists concerned with fundamental cosmic processes or biologists concerned with patterns of evolution, we hear a similar story. The patterns and processes of the world around us are to be understood neither in terms of an unchanging order nor in terms of random disorder, but through a combination of both. In physics, for example, it now appears that there is a fundamental interdependence of chance and necessity. Random and unpredictable events occur in a framework of determined and determining laws. Within this context order can produce novelty and novelty order. We have

> a world whose processes can assemble complexity within a decaying environment and where random events can prove to be the originators of pattern. Such a world is a world of orderliness but not of clockwork regularity, of potentiality without predictability, endowed with an assurance of development but with a certain openness as to its actual form. It is inevitably a world with ragged edges, where order and disorder interlace each other and where the exploration of possibility by chance will lead not only to the evolution of systems of increasing complexity, endowed with new possibilities, but also to the evolution of systems imperfectly formed and malfunctioning. . . The presence in it of physical evils (earthquakes, genetically induced malformations, disease) reflects the untidiness of disorder, just as the presence in it of physical goods (healthy conscious beings, a rich variety of plant and animal life) reflects the organizing power of order.[6]

What seems to hold good at the physical level also seems to hold good at the biological level. Here too there is an interdependence of randomness and order. The survival of chance mutations is determined by the relative fixities of the environment. However, within the patterns of evolution, it has been suggested, three underlying tendencies can be discerned: a tendency of smaller units to combine, a tendency towards greater independence, and a tendency towards a deeper capacity for suffering.[7]

The first two tendencies, although apparently contradictory, are in fact analogous to the movement, through dependence and independence, to interdependence. For example, the individual person becomes more complete a human being in relation to other individual persons. It is the third tendency, however, which is perhaps for our purposes the most suggestive of the three, namely, the tendency towards greater suffering, or vulnerability. Gerd Theissen develops this suggestion:

> All progress has its price. . . . Each step in evolution brought increased suffering. And probably no further progress will be possible without new forms of suffering. . . . Those who have the Spirit articulate the 'sighing of all creation', which runs through the whole of reality as a comprehensive cosmic tendency and which no one can penetrate to the depths. Today the three observable tendencies of evolution towards greater solidarity, responsibility and sensitivity to suffering are all coming together.[8]

If such is the character of the world of which we are a part, a world of trial and error, of becoming expert through experience, a world of increasing responsiveness and responsibility, a world in which openness and vulnerability mark the narrow path that leads to fullness of life, what has this to tell us about the God whose world it is?

A popular picture of God has been one of a God of unchanging and unchangeable power, who by his inscrutable decree orders every detail of what happens in the world. What may look to us like accident or chance is, religiously speaking, to be interpreted as the outcome of divine purpose. Such a picture makes of God an inscrutable monarch, if not a malignant vivisectionist.[9] In reaction against this picture emphasis has more recently been placed on the suffering, or vulnerability, of God. He is with us in the world, alongside us, 'the fellow-sufferer who understands'.[10] So, writing of the Aberfan disaster, W. H. Vanstone could say:

> Our preaching on the Sunday after the tragedy was not of a God who, from the top of the mountain, caused or permitted, for His own inscrutable reasons, its disruption and descent; but of One Who received, at the foot of the mountain, its appalling impact, and Who, in the extremity of endeavour, will find yet new resource to restore and redeem.[11]

The fully trinitarian symbol of God combines order with creativity, purpose with freedom, trustworthiness with patience. God is One who continually creates, redeems and fulfils. In creating he authorizes his creation and gives it authority to be and become itself. He lets it go, accepting the self-limitations which the authority of love requires, making time and space for creatures dependent on himself but with a created reality and independence of their own. The pattern of his creation is one of trial and error, a combination of order and disorder, randomness and necessity. There is no guarantee that things will not 'go wrong'. In fact, there is every indication that things have gone wrong and will continue to go wrong. But that is neither the beginning nor the end of the matter. God also redeems. He places himself alongside his creatures and shares the brokenness of their lives, their hopes and fears. He gives them himself. God also fulfils. What he has to share with his creatures is nothing less than the fullness of his own life. In and through the work of creation and redemption he struggles to elicit from his creatures, singly and together, their deepest potentialities, so that they may enter into the glorious liberty of children of God.

The world we live in is nicely adapted neither to our pleasure nor to our deserts. It is a chancy and risky world. In many ways it is indifferent to our human wants and needs. The fear 'that there is an unbreakable and intimate connection between love and death, between passion and violence, between sex and chaos, between intimacy and destruction of the ego'[12] is only too real a fear. That is how things must have looked from the dereliction of the Cross. But it may just be—as faith, hope and intimations of experience affirm it to be—that the garment of our mortal flesh is being woven by eternal Love, Father, Son, Holy Spirit, and that in the midst of the world's travail, suffering and sin, God rejoices in our happiness rather than our sorrow, our flourishing rather than our diminishment, our life rather than our death.

> Who then devised the torment? Love.
> Love is the unfamiliar Name
> Behind the hands that wove
> The intolerable shirt of flame
> Which human power cannot remove.
> We only live, only suspire
> Consumed by either fire or fire.[13]

NOTES

1. From R. S. Thomas, 'Emerging', in *Late Poems, 1972–82*, Macmillan 1983.
2. J. W. Bowker, 'The Morality of Personal Relationships', in *Making Moral Decisions*, ed. D. M. Mackinnon (SPCK 1969), p.70.
3. See Andrew Henderson, above, pp. 38–9.
4. W. H. Vanstone, *Love's Endeavour, Love's Expense* (Darton, Longman & Todd), p. 99.
5. Austin Farrer, *Love Almighty and Ills Unlimited* (Fontana 1966), p. 13.
6. John Polkinghorne, *Science and Creation* (SPCK 1988), p. 48.
7. See Gerd Theissen, *Biblical Faith: An Evolutionary Approach* (SCM 1988), p.169.
8. ibid., p. 170.
9. See C. S. Lewis, *A Grief Observed* (Faber 1964), p. 26.
10. See, for example, A. N. Whitehead.
11. Vanstone, p. 65.
12. See Sara Maitland, above, pp. 94–5.
13. From T. S. Eliot, 'Little Gidding' in *Collected Poems 1909–62*, Faber 1963.

'And who is my Neighbour?'

(Luke 10.29)

I want to share a story with you, a story from the United States. It's a very simple story about a man called Paul. At the time when it all happened, Paul was in his thirties. Some would say he was a typical middle-class American: he lived in a rich, white suburb on the outskirts of Chicago, in a big respectable suburban house. The house was enormous, beautifully decorated and furnished, with long green lawns reaching down to a tree-lined avenue. It had a wide drive and garaging for two wide American cars. The garage door opened automatically at the flick of a switch.

Paul lived there with Charles, who happened to be Paul's lover. Like Paul, Charles was a successful and rich lawyer. Together they lived a decent law-abiding life: working very hard, enjoying all the benefits of the high salaries and vibrant social lives that their professional status afforded them.

Each evening, Paul would drive home from his office in the centre of Chicago, seated in his large, plush car. He would look down sometimes through the tinted glass of the windows, down onto the houses below the fly-overs along which he sped. He would look down on the crowded streets or at the squalid backs of the tenement blocks where the poor blacks lived, and he would drive on. Paul never ventured into those areas: to be honest, for all his power and his wealth, he was a little afraid of the people that lived down there—afraid of the cultures and lifestyles below that were so different from his own. The places beneath the fly-over he associated with crime, indecency, danger.

He felt much more secure with the broad, well-lit streets of the white suburbs: with his rich, respectable lawyer friends; good, wholesome Americans who earned an honest dollar—like the ones he worshipped with most Sundays at the local church. You could trust them.

One autumn Charles went down suddenly with a 'flu'-like illness which dogged him for weeks. What seemed like flu rapidly became pneumonia, and Charles was hospitalized. Soon after the doctor called Paul in and told him that Charles's immunity system had broken down—that he had AIDS.

Paul was devastated—quite naturally, his world had been turned upside down—the person he loved, with whom he shared his life, had

116

been diagnosed as having a terminal illness. It was not that there were financial worries, both he and Charles could afford all the medical care and attention that would be necessary. It was the sudden emotional need that shocked him. He had never felt helpless before.

Paul felt sure that his church would support them both. He turned hopefully to the pastor, and dutifully the pastor came to their home. But the pastor was very afraid. Paul was not sure whether the pastor was afraid of Charles's illness, or afraid of his love for Charles. But when the pastor came he took the opportunity to give Paul and Charles a piece of his mind, and then he hurried on his way to take a service. He didn't want to come near the situation. Perhaps he wasn't able to.

Paul felt sure this friends would support him: his decent, respectable friends with whom he had always seemed to have so much in common. But when Paul telephoned to tell them the news, they suddenly fell silent, and made excuses about having to rush on to an important meeting. They never called, or visited. Sometimes Paul saw them drive past the house on their way to work. They were so busy.

Suddenly Paul and Charles were very isolated and very alone. One day, in desperation, Paul turned to an organization for people with HIV and their families. A woman called Eunice came to see them at home. She was a black lady, in her fifties. Her son Godwin had suffered with AIDS, and died.

Eunice visited Paul and Charles regularly at home, and in hospital. It was she, and only she, who stuck with Paul through the long painful months of Charles's illness; and when the time came, she did her best to help Paul face life without Charles.

And Paul never forgot her kindness and her lack of fear, nor how one night when he took Eunice home in his car, he found that Eunice lived in a tenement block down under, beneath the fly-overs.

CARA

Care and Resources for people affected by AIDS/HIV

A Pastoral Ministry

Despite its devastation AIDS/HIV Infection has produced creative responses in many places. However, the Church has not always been able to share these positive signs. CARA was launched in July 1988 to bring the resources of spirituality to bear on this problem by . . .

1. Providing pastoral care for people with HIV and AIDS; their relatives and friends; professional and voluntary carers.

2. Creating educational training programmes for people wanting to offer non-judgemental spiritual, emotional and practical support to those affected by HIV/AIDS.

3. Working with other agencies, irrespective of creed or philosophy, engaged in the care of people affected by HIV/AIDS.

4. Theological and spiritual reflection on the issues which HIV/AIDS present both Church and society.

5. The practical use of resources, including buildings, in caring for people with HIV/AIDS.

A Prayer

Living God, source of light and life,
we come to you as broken members
of your body;
your strength is our strength,
your health is our health
and your being is our being.
Grant us your wisdom in our work,
your love in our pain and your
peace in our hearts.

Send your blessing on all those
working with CARA, all those whom
they serve and give us the joy of
everlasting love.

In the name of Jesus your own.

Amen.

Further information: *Fr David Randall, Pastor*
The Basement
178 Lancaster Road
London W11 1QU
Tel. 081 792 8299